THE LIGHT IN THE MIRROR

THE ALBERT E. TURNER FAMILY IN 1919.

Front, left to right: "Billie" Turner, with daughter Doris on her lap, "Mother" Turner, Ruth, Dorothy, with son Chris on her lap, Anna with son Norman. Back: Brinkley Turner, Paul Turner with Paul Egolf, Jr., Albert Jr., Albert E. Turner, Sr., August Tegtmeier with daughter Dora, Paul Egolf, Sr.

THE LIGHT IN THE MIRROR
The Story of Albert E. Turner, Junior

by
Doris Turner Patterson

DORRANCE & COMPANY, INCORPORATED
828 LANCASTER AVENUE • BRYN MAWR, PENNSYLVANIA 19010
Publishers Since 1920

Copyright © 1985 by Doris Turner Patterson
All Rights Reserved
ISBN 0–8059–3001–9
Printed in the United States of America
First Printing

To Gladys
who inspired the best of Albert's life

Contents

ACKNOWLEDGEMENTS	ix
PREFACE	xi
I. Thinking Back	1
II. In Father's Image	5
III. Ties That Bind	15
IV. Odyssey	21
V. Settling Down	29
VI. A Way Out	34
VII. A Need for Healing	40
VIII. On a Wing and a Prayer	44
IX. Many Lifetimes	49
X. Smilin' Al	62
XI. Blessed Are Those	72
XII. Learning, Love, Laughter	79
XIII. Writing and Righting	88
XIV. Revealing the Revelation	99
XV. . . . And There Was Light	110
APPENDIX	116

Acknowledgements

This biography of Albert E. Turner, Jr. was born with the help of a great many people—both his personal friends and others who cared about him.

Gladys Davis Turner is the one without whom it could not have been written at all. She shared not only photographs, papers and letters, but especially her time and memories of deep experiences.

My thanks to Al's Virginia Beach friends and A.R.E. members who offered their feelings on what he had done and what he had meant to them, to Louise Wilson, for the long and lovely letter, to Charlotte and Birley Schoen for their recollections, to Mary Ellen Carter for her description of Al. (I am sorry some who wrote and helped, including Hugh Lynn Cayce and Olive Lander, will not be able to see this book.) Gratitude also goes to Dick Eckenroth, of Swarthmore, and his wife, Mildred, for their assistance.

Special appreciation is due Jeanette Thomas, of the Edgar Cayce Foundation, for her help in checking the Cayce readings quotations. Thanks for background material to William Newlin, for making recordings available, and to Henry George, for the transcripts of his father's sessions with Al.

Thanks also to Juliette Ballard for going over the first part of the manuscript, and to the many others who helped; to Brian Shulik of Dorrance, who spent much personal energy in trying to overcome computer glitches and bring the manuscript together in spite of them.

Thanks to all the family members who responded when asked for help, especially my daughters: Dot, for her insight and assistance and Anne, for her perceptive art work for their great-uncle's story.

The life of one man touches many.

Preface

It wasn't until he was fifty years old that I really began to know my uncle, Albert E. Turner, Jr. As the oldest daughter of his oldest brother, I had grown up with widely varying visions of him: handsome in his Marine uniform, but making Mother very nervous; getting out of his vegetable truck in front of our house to sell apples; talking to Mother's mother about really weird philosophies; the half-heard, scary talk of police, talk of "the black sheep of the Turner family."

But as I began to know him after my father's death, began to see what he was doing at Virginia Beach, what he had gone through and helped others through, I found another man—one with a wealth of sharable experiences, one who had his greatest effect on others after disabling heart attacks and strokes. After his death at Virginia Beach in June of 1968, searching papers and talking with people who knew him there and in Philadelphia, I found more. I sensed a compelling core beneath the actions of Albert the boy, the youth, the man: a deep core of yearning for the revelation and experiencing of God.

"The black sheep of the Turner family" and "the Saint of Virginia Beach" were both the Ulysses of this Odyssey, depending on who was talking about him.

I
Thinking Back

The white ceiling, the beige walls, the movement of white-clad figures around him—Al had no problem realizing that this was a hospital room. The problem was, when a face bent over him and asked a question, he could not seem to respond as he wanted to. Even as he worked his mouth, the sounds that came out were not right. And when the voice said, "Move your hand . . . Move your foot . . ." he tried. He strained. But his muscles weren't listening. It was strange and confusing. Finally the faces receded. The commands stopped. The talking and muttering faded.

As the pain came and went, the people came and went, probing his body, talking to each other, hooking things up, inserting things, removing things.

The one constant was Gladys. She was there, her very presence reassuring. His eyes could find hers, and even if he couldn't get the right words out, she would understand. A small but triumphant thought came to him as he felt the pressure of her hand: they could pray together—and you didn't have to have spoken words for that! He could see the smile on her face and hoped he was smiling back.

Then she was standing. Then bending over him, with a kiss. She had to go home now. Though the doctors didn't have the results of his tests yet, they would surely have them soon. She would be back tomorrow. Meanwhile, he would rest.

ALBERT E. TURNER, JR., it said on the card at the end of the bed, BORN OCT. 21, 1907. That would make him 53 years old in February, 1961.

"Looks in the prime of life," one nurse observed, 'It's a shame. . ."

Though his mind was partly cloudy (had there been a sedative?) Al could catch fragments of the conversations around him. He wanted to reassure the nurse, but no words, only odd sounds, escaped his throat. They checked the tubes running into his arms, patted his shoulder maternally. "Just rest now, Mr. Turner." And they went about their business.

He listened as two doctors talked. "Occlusion of the proximal part

. . . artery, frontal, parietal . . . contralateral hemiplegia. . . ." What it all meant, he could not tell. His heart, of course, was part of the problem. The pain was like that he had felt in those other attacks. How many had there been? Maybe five? But more had happened than just the heart pain. He was a little afraid to think about it. The trouble was, when you couldn't move anything but your eyes and mouth, there wasn't much else to do *but* think.

He couldn't direct his body anymore. Could he direct his thoughts?

INTERLUDE

April 18, 1920.

Al was only twelve when Father died. Twelve—that age when you're neither fish nor fowl nor good red herring. That age when, if anything is ever going to go wrong, it will start. When the hurts are twice their size, and the buffers are paper thin.

But there wasn't anything he could do about it. Father was gone. Al felt the ache, like a big, cold thumb, pushing all along his spine.

All the relatives there there—Aunt Maude, Uncle George, Uncle John, even Aunt Catherine, who wasn't a real aunt but sure talked like one. All of them kept talking, words of sympathy making X's in the air, crosscurrents, confusion.

"A great man—more than that, a good man," the minister had said. The words had rippled through the pool of conversation. "Now God has taken him." The ripples widened. Al felt he had to get out of this sea of persons, this flood of words. He slipped away from the talkers.

If God had taken Father, and Al knew that God and Father were very close, it had to be for something glorious. Father always insisted on the Ten Commandments. Father made wonderful prayers, not just for grace at the table but for special times. Al had listened in awe when Father talked to God, talked about the Power and the Glory. Al had this tender, fearful yearning to glimpse a bit of the glory.

He tiptoed upstairs, past the bedrooms, to the door to the attic— up the long, steep stairway to the attic, where he could be alone, and ask if God could show him a little glimpse, a sign, of His glory and of Father. As he came up into the attic, he smelled the mothballs, the dry wood, the restful oldness.

In the dimness, his heart thudded. Suddenly a tingling went through every vein. A light had flashed. Al looked towards a curtain across the areaway. Mother had been stretching curtains; she had hung some up before storing them. Behind the curtain was this light, this beaming—this something strange and wonderful.

Al hesitated. *Something* was there! Was it the Revelation? The light seemed to move. He prayed, and drew closer. Something glimmered behind the curtain. Did he dare to pull it away and look?

He reached his fingers out to the folds of the curtain and—

A dim face stared at him while the light of the little attic window shone over his shoulder, in the tall mirror, the old pierglass. It had been his own movement between the light and the curtain-shrouded mirror that had produced the moving light.

The Revelation?

"It's only me," he whispered soundlessly. At first he had felt with his whole being as if he had been close to the Revelation of God. Now his heart didn't thud, it just ached. His hot, teary eyes knew what they saw. His lips moved again: "It's only me."

***

Al's mind could visit the past then return to the frustrating present. Day blurred into night and back to day. Nurses probed and pushed and pulled and questioned. Doctors shone lights, tapped, probed and questioned. They demanded answers Al struggled in vain to give. There were times it was good for his mind to slip away to the past.

. . .

But whenever Gladys came in, he returned glady to the present. As he lay there watching her, statuesque even at fifty-six, her blue eyes bright with a special warmth, he knew she was really an angel, an angel of mercy. He wanted to tell her. But he couldn't. Yet she seemed to know, she showed it with her smile, her musical laugh, her squeeze of his hand.

Finally the doctors presented Gladys with the results of their tests. Her husband had had not just a heart attack (his sixth) but a severe stroke which had left him more than half paralyzed, barely able to function. With luck and much therapy, she might look forward eventually to pushing him around in a wheelchair. Albert Turner would never walk again. They implied, without being specific, that there were many other things he'd probably never do again. He had had a stroke before, but not as severely crippling as this one. As to how much of his brain function he had left, one doctor shook his head. "I can't really promise anything . . ."

Gladys left them and came back to Al; she smiled and grasped his hand tightly in hers. "We'll do the best we can."

Cards and letters began flowing into the hospital room, from Al's frields in the Norfolk Post Office where he had worked, from his neighbors, and especially from his friends from the Association for Research and Enlightenment (A.R.E.). (There were very few in the A.R.E. Headquarters at Virginia Beach who did not know Al, none who did not know Gladys. Nearly everyone who had ever heard of Edgar Cayce, whose psychic readings formed the basis of study for the A.R.E.—and that included many thousands—knew that Gladys Davis had been the one who sat at the "sleeping prophet's" side and wrote down, then transcribed his trance readings, over 14,000 of them. They knew she was the secretary of the A.R.E. and of the Edgar Cayce Foundation, which had continued growing since Mr. Cayce's death in 1945.)

Of course Gladys was still very active. But Al, imprisoned in the helpless body, had many hours when he could only rest and remember.

II
In Father's Image

As a child, Al believed God was made in Father's image. Father. Albert Edward Turner. Al carried that name like a badge of honor, with "Jr." added—but also with the uneasy feeling that the older children didn't think he deserved it. Grandpa Charles Brinkley Turner, the old leather merchant, had named his firstborn "Albert Edward" after the young Prince of Wales. And Father had often been called a "prince among men."

Al, born in 1907, was the youngest of the six Turner children, the baby of the family. Still he had been aware, from the time he could identify visitors, that a great many people thought Father was great. Father had been one of the founders of Philadelphia's "Committee of Seventy," seventy citizens who volunteered their time to overseeing the city government to help keep it honest and efficient. Turner Street in Philadelphia was named for him.

When Richard Blankenburg was Mayor of Philadelphia, it was truly the City of Brotherly Love for him and Father. They were like affectionate brothers, embracing each other when they met, and even, in their letters, calling each other "Beloved." Other friends included Pennsylvania's Governor Brumbaugh, and publisher Cyrus H. K. Curtis, who several times invited Father for trips on his yacht. Al had enjoyed the photographs Father sent home from his trips.

Father had radiated a vitality that seemed to grow from being involved with others' lives. He was constantly active, not just with his work—he had been Financial Editor of the old *North American*, he had written a financial column for the *Evening Bulletin*, and with his friend Clarence Harper, he had started the investment firm of Harper and Turner—but also with putting his faith into action. He was always doing something with the Methodist Episcopal Church, with the Young Men's Christian Association, and with the Christian Businessmen's Association. When World War I had spread hunger through Europe, he had helped send food supplies abroad. Herbert Hoover, in charge of that relief, wrote him personal thanks.

Al could recall the day in March, 1915, even though he was only a boy of seven, when father's fiftieth birthday was celebrated with a banquet at the City Club, with almost every city dignitary and many a state official on hand to do him honor. In his scrap book, Al had kept a copy of that banquet program, as he had kept copies of many of Father's poems. So many people wanted copies of Father's poems! The poem "If One Believes" was in such demand that a "cut" of brass was made from Father's handwriting, so when more requests came in the "cut" was inked, pressed on paper and presto! More "handwritten" copies to give.

Philadelphia for Albert E. Turner had been a city of brotherly love, of praise and honor. For Albert E. Turner Jr.?

There really had been seven Turner children. The first had died at birth. Charles Brinkley Turner, named for his grandfather, became the oldest; then Dorothy Mason, Anna Brown, Paul Flagler, Ruth Margaret, and finally little Albert, Junior.

For the family, Father was king, loving ruler, religious head. Father's word was law, and the law included the Ten Commandments. How lucky they were to live with such godly guidance—weren't they?

Sundays for example . . .

Sundays were special days. The Sabbath, it was drilled into the Turner children, was to be kept solely for worship, for behavior pleasing to the Lord.

"Why can't we read the comic pages, Father? Jimmy Michaels's family does!"

"Albert!" His tone was firm. "It is enough that I say so. But I will remind you that the Bible tells us, 'Remember the sabbath day, to keep it holy.' Where is that verse found, Albert, boy?" Father finished gently.

Al felt the lump rise in his throat as Father's tone lowered.

"The Ten Commandments, Father. It is the fourth."

Inside, he burned with that little flame of pain that came with Father's religious correction.

Now Father's voice rose with righteous thunder. "There is *nothing* holy about the comics! Repeat that, Albert."

And Al had repeated it, face flushed, turning away from the folded newspaper that would stay folded until Monday. Those funny black-and-orange drawings of Maggie and Jiggs, of the Katzenjammer Kids, of Happy Hooligan—they weren't holy and could not be read on Sunday.

Sunday always began with Sunday School at the Methodist Episcopal Church. The whole family went, starched and shiny, to their respective classes. Father was much in demand; often he was asked to teach the Men's Bible Class. It was 'Please, Albert,' and 'Would you, Mr. Turner?' and Father's gentle, knowing answers. Father was even elected President of the Laymen's Association of the Philadelphia Conference. In the church, too, people looked up to him.

Father, Albert knew, was close to God. When Father prayed it wasn't just words; he really talked to God. He let the family know, if there were any doubt, that God was listening. Albert was alive because of that. Seven years old and full of energy, he had been playing, chasing the ball in the sunny street, in the Overbrook section of Philadelphia where they lived. He never saw the motor car swing around the corner. He heard it coming, of course, but had thought nothing of it because they usually went straight ahead instead of turning. After the first stars of pain there had been this strange dream of wrestling with a kind of cloudy spirit, wrestling that ended when the mists cleared a little and Father's and Mother's faces hung above him. Later, he learned he had been in a coma nearly four days, that the neighbors, even people who had only read about the accident in the newspaper, had been praying for him.

"The Lord heard our prayers, Albert darling," Mother assured him, night after night, "We must thank Him for His mercy!" They all agreed that God had done it, God had worked a miracle with Albert. The doctors didn't think the little boy would live. Yet because Father and Mother prayed, here he was, getting better every day.

Even after the pain subsided, and the words "concussion" and "possible brain damage" were no longer whispered, Al still enjoyed unusual attention and affection. No more was he at the mercy of the governess, who had sometimes shut him in a closet if he didn't eat his meal. Now the convalescent had only to ask for something and they would hurry to bring it.

Before, his brother Paul had been the shining favorite of Father and Mother. Now Paul kept coming to Al, trying to comfort and amuse him. Ruthie, instead of teasing him, brought him broth and cookies. Even Brinkley had come home from Haverford college, and Dot and Nan (which was what her family and friends called Anna) from Bryn Mawr College, to give him extra smiles and attention. It felt good—really good—while it lasted.

Brink, too, had felt the force of Father's word, but in a different way. Even though Brink was a college man now, Father had made it clear his word was law for everyone under his roof. Brink had come home for a fall weekend. Al remembered waking up, that chill Saturday night, when he heard a knocking on the front door. Looking out the window, Al saw his big brother, who had been out with a friend for the evening. If no one else heard the knocking, Al would let Brink in; he started to hurry downstairs. But Father met him in the hallway and stopped him.

"Go back to bed, Albert!"

"But Father, Brink is outside."

"Your brother was told to come home before midnight. It is now twenty minutes past midnight. He has made his choice."

"But—"

"TO BED!" Father thundered, and Al trudged miserably back to his room. He peered through the window and watched his oldest brother slowly walking off into the darkness. Something in him ached.

But there were good times, warm times, wonderful times, as well: the Christmas mornings when Father had the whole family line up outside the living room where the presents were all piled. Then one behind the other they would walk in singing "Silent Night," and complete the last line of the carol before diving to their gifts with delighted cries. The rides in Father's new motor car, which sometimes went even faster than fifteen miles an hour. Sunday walks in Cobbs Creek Park in the springtime, when Father would call each tiny flower by name, and tell them about the marvels of nature, about finding "tongues in trees, books in the running brooks/Sermons in stones, and God in everything." (Later Al found Shakespeare had said, "and good in everything," but Father's quotation stood.)

At the Sunday School picnics, Father was on hand often, with his straw hat tilted and eyes a-twinkle, sometimes leading the songs, coaxing choruses even from the quiet ones. But not in the baseball games. Al recalled the time father hit the ball and started to run—then stumbled, turning white. Two of the men had led him back to the bench, and Uncle John had insisted it was time to go home, even though the game was nowhere near over. Al knew something serious was wrong when the doctor came. But father was up and around again, and the grownups did not discuss it in front of "the children." But Father did no more running, after that.

Worry about Father was fading when Paul—Paul, who almost never complained of anything—felt too sick to go to school. At first it seemed just an upset stomach and fever, but soon his temperature rose so high

Mother was frightened. She called Father. Father called Dr. Talley, who confirmed their fears: it was acute appendicitis. In spite of all the treatment, the fever rose, delirium came. Al saw Father and Mother bending over Paul's bed, and ran to join them. They were praying, and he prayed with them, "Heavenly Father, have mercy on Paul. Let him feel thy healing love." Slowly, Paul's delirium began to abate. Hour after hour Al would watch by Paul's bed, and when his beloved brother was thirsty, Al would run to the icebox, grab the icepick and chip off tiny pieces from the big block, then bring them to Paul so he could suck them. Al would sit with Paul and coax him. "Think about the winter. Think about the snow—that'll make you feel cool! I heard Father say you might get a new sled!" And Paul would smile faintly.

Sure enough, Paul gradually recovered, and the snow did come, and the new sled with it. There were many hills around Overbrook, and up them Al would trudge behind his favorite brother. There was an especially nice one the other side of City Line Avenue, where Al would lie on top of Paul on the sled and they would glide, the fast snow hissing in their ears, seeming to head straight for the rocky stream at the bottom. Then they would turn just in time to miss the stream and coast for yards along the meadow.

Only when Paul was around did Al really have fun playing. He had no close friends from school, and as for the rest of his family, Brinkley was spending most of his free time with his fiancee Billie Savage, his sister Dot was planning a wedding too; even Nan was casting eyes at Brinkley's friend Paul Egolf, and as for his sister Ruth, just a bit older than he, she was at the age when older boys looked interesting but younger ones, especially brothers, were anathema.

The snow melted, the sun warmed Overbrook, and the bicycles came out. Al loved riding on the handlebars with Paul, who would cry, "Hi-Yo, Al boy, here we go!" and they'd swoop down Woodbine Avenue, sometimes even faster than a motorcar.

When school was out, they would pack up and the whole family would take the train to Pocono Summit and then the "station wagon" to Pocono Pines and a small bus to Pocono Lake Preserve, where the Turners had Tamarack Camp. (All the families who belonged to the Preserve called their houses in the pine woods "camps"; the first homes there actually had been the tents used while the men were building the houses.) Tamarack Camp included two gray cottages, nested in pines and mountain maples, alongside Tamarack Trail: the larger cottage nearer the lake, the part called Veery Cove, and the smaller one farther up the hill.

"Pocono" was another world. Tall firs and maples gave thick shade in the day and scary silhouettes against the sky at night. Father spent as much of the time as he could spare from his business there with the family. He would take the children out in the rowboat, fishing, teaching them—even Ruth—to bait a hook, cast a line, and wait in silence while the water rippled invitingly. They yelped with delight when a perch or even a sunnie was flipped into the bucket between the seats.

Father taught the children to swim, rewarded them with a shiny penknife when they could splash doggie-paddle around the Turner dock. Then when they could swim breast stroke or the trudgeon (also called the "Australian crawl") and could make the hundred yards across the cove to the White dock, they could count on a new bicycle. The *only* way his children would get a bicycle.

At "Pocono" too were the long magic walks with Father up the Tamarack Trail, sometimes with berry pails, looking especially for the large, sweet "high bush" blueberries in the swampy areas, and also the huckleberries which they learned to strip off the low bushes much as a farmer strips milk from a cow's udder. It was a rite of summer, stripping the bushes, hearing the berries plop into the pail, smelling their sweetness in the sun, munching a handful when no one was looking.

Nature magic enhanced their hikes; Father showed them the fringed gentian, the Indian paintbrush and, with a chuckling shudder, the devil's paintbrush. He'd offer them a sprig of wintergreen and they'd chew the shiny leaf, savoring the flavor long after. They learned to know the hemlock, red spruce, black spruce, and always paused a respectful moment by the towering white pine called the Iroquois. Another mile up the trail brought them to crystal clear Wolf Run, where they would kneel on a mossy rock and sip the icy ripples for their thirst. Then up the rhododendron-shaded corduroy road to the remains of a log cabin. Father described and Al pictured the old settler who had laid those logs across the trail, driving his wagon over this bumpy wooden road and on across the next mountain and over to Wilkes-barre, every couple of months, for his bags of flour and salt and coal oil for his lamps. The old settler's cabin seemed to be sleeping with parted logs under the apple tree, which kept bringing out its apples obediently, years after the man who planted it had passed on.

The most fascinating of the trips with Father was the once-a-year hike, which only the sturdier ones could take, to that mysterious place called "Lost Lake," where not one civilized trail approached. They had to find it by wood craft. Of course there was a trail part of the way. But then they broke through the woods, with Father leading, making occasional blazes with his knife on the tree trunks so they could find the way again. What a place, once they did reach the shore of that strange lake with no visible inlet or outlet! The shore was like no other shore they'd seen; it looked like soft moss and bushes, but when you jumped, the bushes and nearby trees jumped too! If you stamped hard, your foot could go right through the moss to the icy water below. If you should step off the edge of the shore, you'd go straight down! Father pushed a long branch deep into the dark lake; it wasn't long enough to touch the bottom. Strange plants, even a Venus's flytrap, flourished along the springy banks.

During these summers at Pocono Lake Preserve the whole family seemed to grow stronger, absorbing some of the essence of the forests and lake, before the arrival of September meant they had to return to Philadelphia.

But the summer of 1916 was different: the Turner family that had stayed together, had prayed together and played together was together now only at rare intervals. Brinkley had married the girl who had been Dot's roommate at Bryn Mawr College, Billie Savage, and Brinkley and Billie had their own home in Narberth. Dot had married that tall, thin civil engineer, August Tegtmeier; they were living in Lansdowne. Nan was married to Paul Egolf, and lived in Narberth too. The only ones left were Ruth, who was planning to go to art school, Paul, starting high school, and Al. So it was really up to him and Paul to keep the family traditions going, Al felt.

But sadly, even at Pocono Paul, too, had less time to spend with his little brother. He often went hiking with other friends, leaving Al behind. Sometimes Al sneaked away to follow them. Hidden by a sassafras bush, he would watch them—growing lonelier the more he saw the older boys enjoying themselves. Then bad luck struck Paul. He developed an abscessed tooth. Vividly Al remembered how Paul's face swelled to a painful, unnatural size. But because there was no dentist at the Preserve, Mother had to go in the rowboat to the office at the far end of the lake and arrange to hire a car to take Paul fifty miles to reach the dentist.

Times should have been better when school started again, but there was a feeling of tenseness in the air. There was talk of the Kaiser and U-Boats and how bad it was for the Allies. Then the U-Boats sank the Lusitania, and finally, on April 6, 1917, the United States declared war on the Kaiser. Father gathered the children together. "Every one of us wants to serve his country," he said. Although he could not go overseas and fight, with Harper and Turner working for the Liberty Loan drive they would be helping their country all the same. To Father's delight, Paul entered wholeheartedly into the drive to sell Liberty Bonds. Al was "too young."

Paul had some magic about him that made people laugh when he smiled, that made them want what he wanted, that made them say "Yes" when he asked. That was how Paul earned the almost inconceivable sum of $77,000 for the Third Liberty Loan, and they called Paul to the platform at City Hall to give him a medal. Of course all the Turner family was there. As his brother stepped forth, Al turned to the people behind him and proudly announced, "That's my brother!"

Though there were grand moments like that, still it seemed as if there were so little time left to share, as if some conspiracy were trying to pull the people Al loved farther and farther away from him.

Peace was announced—the false peace in late October, 1918, and the real peace on November 11, with the signing of the Armistice. Bells clanged in the church towers and fire houses, and people ran into the streets and hugged each other, friends and strangers alike.

But peace was not in Mother's eyes when she looked at Father. He didn't look very different, Al thought, just thinner, more easily tired.

It was Paul, though, who came down with pneumonia, double pneumonia. As Paul lay there, feverish, struggling to breathe, Al held onto his brother's limp hand and whispered to him, "When you're better, we're going to go off on our own, just us!" Paul nodded faintly. "Where it's sunny and warm," Al went on, as the December wind muttered against the shutters, "we'll lie on the beach, under palm trees, in Cuba and places like that . . ."

The need to get away loomed larger, fed by the fear that he and Paul might become trapped like Brinkley, Nan and Dot, fenced in with babies and a job that meant one place, one town. Paul listened to Al describing faraway places and smiled. But as he gradually regained his strength, he reminded his little brother, "We've got responsibilities, you know. Mother and Father want us to go to college. And Father doesn't look so strong these days so they might need us."

"But Paul, you promised!"

"After college, then, Al boy, we'll see the world—all of it!"

But as the months went on, Al began to fear even his brother Paul wouldn't go with him. Paul had only one more year at Central High School, and he kept going to one activity and then another after school without even a mention to Al, not even a hint of an invitation.

Father and Mother finally took a trip together, to Hawaii, the next year, 1919. Their letters home brought such news, such pictures, that Al wanted more than ever to break away and travel. The most pictures, the warmest news, came in the letters for Paul, but there were other letters for Al and Ruth. Then the travelers returned with the curious souvenirs, the coconut head, the strangely woven basket, the oddities that fascinated.

And Father took a trip on a steamer to Panama, where they were building the canal that would connect two oceans. Al and Ruth and Paul listened eagerly as Mother read the letters, and they looked with amazement at the postal cards and the post-card sized photographs he sent showing the men digging the "big ditch."

Adventures *were* possible. Father was living them. Al wanted and needed to share adventures, but there was no way he could share Father's. He wanted to share Paul's when they were again at Pocono. Sometimes Paul would take his little brother along. But there were other times, like the sunny July day Paul and three friends packed their lunches and set off on a hike across the mountain. They clearly didn't want him. Biting back tears, Al watched them leave, then quickly grabbed some bread and a piece of chicken from the ice box and set off, trailing the others like an Indian. He followed them up the trail, across a meadow, through the brush along the stream, to the overlook by the towering pine. Al watched his brother laughing, tossing a ball with his friends, sharing with *them*—and put his face to the moss on the large cool rock beside him and let the hurt wash over him. Late in the day, long after the others returned, he came back.

That winter the Turner house on Woodbine Avenue no longer echoed with laughter and challenges for sled races and snowball fights. Something in Mother's face when she looked at Father hushed the laughter. Al felt a chill in the air that had nothing to do with the temperature, a muted, wordless fear. "What's wrong?" he asked Mother. "Nothing," was the artificial answer. Al had taken piano lessons, and tried to dispel the tension by playing. Father, who was home more often now, encouraged Al to play for him, especially his favorite hymn, "The Son of God Goes Forth to War." Al and Paul and Ruth would join in; Father's eyes would light up, his own voice ring out with fervor.

One April Sunday when Brinkley and Billie and Paul and Nan were there too for a family dinner, Father was especially anxious to hear everyone sing. All joined around the piano, and the chorus rang, "We'll follow in His train!"

Father's grace before the meal was especially moving. No set words, but as the spirit moved him, he called on God to bless the family circle. It was almost as if the food was the Communion bread. The roast and mashed potatoes and gravy had just been served, when Father suddenly leaned back, as if gasping, then slid from his chair. Al sat frozen to his chair as Brinkley bent over Father, and loosened his tie. Mother rushed to his side. The eyes were open wide but no breath or voice. They called his name, then "Dear God!" They carried him into the living room. Al prayed as hard as he knew. Paul telephoned the doctor, his voice breaking. The doctor came—but Father's heart had given out.

Father was the man who could speak with God! He was the one who had prayed and persuaded God that Paul and even he, Albert should live when they might have died. Father was so close to God he was bound up with God, and where Father went, God would go also.

At West Laurel Hill Cemetery, Al saw them lower Father into the ground.

III
Ties That Bind

Beliefs are what you build your life on. If something puts a crack in your belief you need to patch it, or else your life might fall apart.

After Father's death Al kept hoping for some kind of sign, a gleam from the sky or a rainbow perhaps, to show him God and Father were together, that his prayers were being heard. But, except for that one time in the attic when he thought he'd seen a spirit but it was just the light reflection in the old mirror, nothing different happened.

Things had to keep going the way they were when Father was alive.

But they didn't. The atmosphere in the Turner house had changed. No bursts of laughter. No songs—certainly not "The Son of God Goes Forth to War." No kidding around, even with the older brothers and sisters who had often kidded before. Even Mother had begun to change. Al recalled how she had stood stately at Father's side, a gentlewoman and queen of her household. Now that gentleness was put aside. Mother was a matriarch. Mother was a director. Mother called family councils; she insisted on everyone, even the married children, being present and carrying out the tasks she assigned them.

At Father's funeral, Mother had held tight to Paul and Al and told them, "You are my men now. I depend on you." But it was not just on them, it was on everyone in the family that she depended. In no uncertain terms she spelled out for each his responsibilities. It seemed clear that she knew her security was not in what Father had left her. With any mistakes in management, that could disappear overnight. Her security lay in her own wits and in her children's cooperation.

Brinkley was given responsibility for helping with her accounts and taxes. Billie, the only woman in the family who knew how to drive, had the duty to drive Mother where she needed to go: errands, and of course, regular trips to Father's grave.

Dorothy helped with the sewing and mending; August, with his civil engineer's background, helped with advice and repair of the Overbrook house they were soon to sell.

Anna would see to all Mother's correspondence and social plans; her husband Paul, however, was usually walled in his favorite world of model trains when he was not on the reporter's beat for the *Public Ledger* or the *Associated Press*.

Al's brother Paul had been accepted at Haverford College, and nothing, Mother felt, should interfere with his preparation for it.

Ruth was usually drawing or painting, intently self-absorbed. Still, she had a large share of the housework, held to it by Mother's watchful eye.

And Al?—all the miscellaneous short errands, and the yard work. Mother's sharp eyes spotted any and everything needing attention; she assigned lists of daily chores.

Was this really the same Mother who had comforted them when there was a broken arm or even a skinned knee? who had tended them carefully when they were under the quilts with a fever? who had laughed and joked and played with her children?

After one particularly sharp conference, when the married children had left and the harsh voices ceased, Al found Mother leaning against the back of the sofa, her eyes closed. She didn't look like a matriarch. She looked exhausted. Her eyes opened.

"What is it, Albert?"

In his changing voice, he asked with a quaver, "Are you all right?"

The firm expression on her face suddenly melted; her eyes held pleading. Her voice started calmly, "I'm fine, thank you—" then broke.

"Oh, Albert!" She reached out and took her fourteen-year-old in her arms. "My son, my baby," she murmured.

Time seemed to stand still for the two of them.

Then Mother began to tell him softly that she realized things had changed, but if he could know some other things—about her mother and about his father—perhaps he would understand why.

"My mother, Sarah Flagler Botsford, told me about her own growing up. I typed the story and will give you a copy of it some day. Her family sent her older sister to a fine boarding school and had no money left for her. So her father arranged with the school for her to work her way through, cleaning the bedrooms and lavatories."

"Even the toilets?" Al could not imagine his grandmother, whom he faintly remembered with lace and sachet, as a little girl scrubbing basins.

Mother ignored the question. "When she graduated, she obtained a position as a school teacher in a one-room schoolhouse in northern New York. She had to clean the schoolroom and fire up the coal stove before eight o'clock in the morning, then teach all the grades—until the last desk and board was cleaned up around half-past four in the afternoon. For this she was paid $1.50 a week—but she had to pay $1.00 of that for her board and room."

"Grandma did that?"

Mother shook her head slightly. "The way her life was, Albert, someone else was always running it. The town where she taught would not allow any school teacher to see any gentlemen friends; of course she could not be married. When finally she did fall in love with a young man, her father said he was not suitable for her and her family forbade her to see him. She felt very sad, but she did not dare to oppose them. Then they eventually chose for her a prosperous widower."

"Grandpa Botsford?" Al had only the faintest recollection of the white-haired old man.

"They named their first daughter Artemisia, after his first wife," Mother went on as if not hearing him. Al had a faint idea of what it might be like to have your oldest child named after your husband's first wife. "And so I knew what a blessing it was for me, after hearing what my mother had to do, that I was able to go to a nice school and not have to clean the rooms and lavatories, to be able to decide for myself what position to look for. After I graduated from the Lockport School I went to work in an office."

Al sat up and looked at his mother. "They called me a 'typewriter'," she went on, then laughed at the expression on his face. "Yes, that was the name they gave to the women who operated one of Mr. Remington's typing machines." Her father had been shocked, but not as shocked as the neighbors, when Dora Botsford had not stayed home to teach piano but had gone to work in an office among *men*. Dora was determined to be independent—but religious as well. "The Lord was with me. He gave me strength," she sighed, and then her eyes began to twinkle. "So when the young men began courting me, I knew the man I married would have to be strong. I was a strong woman, I could tell people what to do and they would do it. But the Bible says the man shall be head of the family." A smile touched the corners of her mouth.

"Finally I had to decide between two men—one was a businessman who was doing a lot of work with the YMCA, and the other was a minister. It was so hard to decide between them! Then I found a night when they both had engagements, and I invited each of them to dinner that night." She chuckled. "The minister broke his engagement to come to dinner with me."

Al had known father was very religious but hadn't realized he was a minister.

"So I chose the *other* man!" she laughed.

Al gasped, then laughed too. It was becoming clearer; mother had deliberately chosen a man who would not let her influence him to break his word to someone else. She knew her own strength and she wanted a man who would be stronger. Father had been. Like a rock. Like iron. And now he was gone. Indeed, Mother did seem to be a natural director. With nothing now to stop her.

The house at 6435 Woodbine Avenue in Overbrook was sold, and Mother, Paul, Ruth and Al moved into a new home on Berkely Road in Haverford, only a short walk from Haverford College, where Paul was now a student.

The fact that Paul was able to live on campus, which was fine for Paul, increased Al's sense of change and loneliness. Ruth went off to art school, and Al was the only child at home. He had not had many friends going to school in Overbrook, and of course the change to Lower Merion High School meant even fewer. It would not have been so bad if he could have spent a lot of time with his favorite brother, but Paul's free time didn't often fit Al's afterschool hours. Happily there were some occasions when Al could walk over to Haverford College and meet his brother and grin when Paul introduced him to his friends.

"Watch out for this whiz, when he comes along," Paul would say and give Al a proud slap on the back.

April, 1922.

What a glorious spring it turned out to be! After the dull brown winter, crocuses popped their lavenders and yellows up through the grass almost overnight. The forsythia around the house seemed to spray gold blossoms. Warming breezes brought the scent of wanderlust. All around were new buds, new births, tiny peepers in robins' nests, baby squirrels. And not just nature. Al was already an uncle six times, and now Nan and Billie and Dot all promised he'd be one again. Instead of exciting him, this building up of family ties seemed threatening—as if these ties could become a rope to bind him down, to keep him and Paul from the wanderings, the Odyssey, the adventures he'd been dreaming about, adventures with far more fascination than his high school future. It was hard to hit the books these days. Still, he made the effort. Paul and Mother were counting on him.

On his way up Berkely Road, Al thought of the good news he was bringing: an A in a math test—thanks largely to Paul's help. That would cheer Mother up, too.

But why were people going into and out of the house? Had something happened to Mother? Al broke into a run.

In the living room, Mother was sitting back in her chair while a strange woman held smelling salts. Two men from the college were there, looking terrible, saying something incomprehensible. And Brinkley, who should have been at work, was here, talking to the men, looking as terrible as they did. Something had to be very wrong. But if it was wrong, why wasn't Paul there? He was the one everyone had always counted on—Paul with the merry smile, Paul with the cool head.

"Where's Paul?"

Their eyes turned towards him; their eyes carried the message. Brinkley's lips formed the words. But it was impossible. It couldn't be.

"No!" the cry broke from his throat. "No! There's got to be a mistake!"

But there wasn't.

It had been a freak accident. A friend practicing a swing with his golf club had swung it behind him. Paul hadn't seen it. It had caught him on the head. His friend and others had come to the house, weeping. Somehow, he, Mother, everyone—they were all comforting each other. They had all loved Paul. The tears were like rain on plants in spring snow: they kept the numbing grief from chilling everything.

Then the formalities, the doctor and the certificates and the funeral. So many of the Haverford men at the funeral! They drove to West Laurel Hill Cemetery where Paul was laid beside his father in the family plot. The new leaves on the Japanese maple, the fresh flowers in their containers, were mocking. Nothing could ever be truly alive again.

As they went through the motions of living during the following weeks, Al noticed Mother seemed wrapped up in her loss. Friends from Haverford College would stop by the house; they, too, were concerned. Several were not only friends, but Friends—members of the Society of Friends, or Quakers. (Haverford, after all, was a Quaker college.) These men spoke of peace of mind and heart, and how there was "that of God in every man."

Father, too, had thought highly of the Quakers; that was one reason he had chosen the Quaker community, Pocono Lake Preserve, for their summer vacations. Al recalled also how Rufus Jones had come to dinner one evening. There was a strength and calm about these Friends.

But it was not enough for healing. Al ached in heart and soul but he kept going to school. Mother wept and kept going to the cemetery. Every day. Of course it was Billie, Brink's wife, who had to drive Mother there. Even though Billie was in the last months of her third pregnancy, Mother insisted on going daily to the graves of those two she missed so much. Billie, Al noticed, looked as wan as Mother. Was that what happened when you stayed around graves?

IV

Odyssey

Monday, June 16, 1924.

The sun was bright and the locusts were singing. The sky gleamed with June polish rubbed in by the breezes, fragrant with sweet-grass and clover. Al adjusted the big cardboard sign on his back so that motorists approaching from behind him could read:

> HIGHWAY
> PHILA. TO FRISCO
> HOW ABOUT A LIFT?

A Reo went by. Then a Studebaker. The driver gave him a grin and a wave, but kept on going.

School was out.

Friday night, Al had gone to the stage of Lower Merion High School and received his diploma from the principal, Mr. Pennypacker. The orchestra had sawed away at Valse Ballet. Marcus Goulding had lauded "Lincoln and the Constitution." They had prated aboout the virtues of all the prize winners. Al thought of how Paul had said he would come to his graduation, and was very nearly sick in his seat.

He had tossed his cap, his "mortarboard," in the air with the others, but instead of going out to celebrate he had gone back home with Mother.

She had made a ceremony out of it. She had brought out the teakwood box. In the box was a brown, bulging bag. Mother lifted it out with both hands.

"Albert, your Father and I planned for your college education. After he died, I continued saving, and I knew every penny would add up. I have counted them. There are forty thousand pennies here, four hundred dollars. That four hundred dollars will see you into Haverford College. You will be able to add to it from your own earnings for the rest of your needs. Here it is, Son."

With shaking hands Al took the heavy bag, nearly dropping it, while his feelings churned within him. Mother, his brother Brink, his sister Dot, his sister Nan, all were counting on him to go to college too. And Father would have wanted it. (Everyone had always taken Father for a college-educated man, though it was his manner and his knowledge of great books that gave the impression. But if you were to stand out in the business world, it was an impression you needed to make.) They all expected him to follow the pattern. But he could feel the pattern tearing inside him.

He held out the bag. "No, Mother. I can't—"

When her hands didn't move, he put the bulging sack back in the teakwood box and closed the lid.

She was incredulous. "How do you intend to go—?"

Looking down to avoid her eyes, he tried to explain. "I don't, Mother. I don't intend to go. Please try to understand. College is—its—" But he could only stutter. He could not get the truth out.

"Albert, dear—"

"I can't, Mother."

Her eyes flashed. Her mouth drew a thin, pained line. "Would you disappoint your father?"

That hurt. He turned and went to his room, to his bed, pounding the pillow with clenched fists. Let her think what she liked, it would only wound her worse if he told her the real reason. College meant friends and plans and ideals of Father, and Father was dead. College meant friends and plans and ideals of Paul. And Paul was dead. He and Paul had made plans to see the world. Paul was dead. He could picture Mother's hand in a velvet glove pointing the way into a cage lined with tombstones.

Al had packed his knapsack with some bread, some cheese, changes of clothing and a blanket, and filled a canteen with water. He told her the next morning, "I have to go." She looked at him but it was as if she didn't really see him. "I'll write," he said. She shook her head. He closed the door slowly.

He had to get out. To get away. To taste the life beyond the heatwaves on the macadam, past Overbrook, Merion, Ardmore, Haverford, Bryn Mawr, Paoli, Malvern, Lancaster—

. . . to forget how mother had tried to beg him to stay without seeming to beg, had tried to hold him by the invisible chains she had forged. It was hard, it did hurt. He knew she loved him and he loved her—but he had to get out or die inside.

He was picked up by the twenty-ninth car to come by: people who had no idea that he had Albert E. Turner for his father, and who probably would not have cared if they had known, people who knew only that he was young and headed west.

Al kept a careful journal of his trip, noting that he had started out with "the immense sum of forty-five dollars . . . the saving from a year's toil at all sorts of odd jobs." This was his own money, not his mother's; this was his own journey, no one else's; the experiences to come would be his, not his father's or his brothers'.

"Passing through the Forest Reservation at Caledonia I was delighted by the sweet-scented pines. It would have made an excellent place to lay down my blanket (for I carried a blanket and pack with necessities), but it was not late enough."

"At Chambersburg I mailed some post cards. I had some trouble getting my paraphernalia inside the corridor of the post office, and a man standing there helped me. He then gave me two pamphlets on "How to Get to Heaven" and a ten cent piece. I accepted this money, of course, knowing that I would need all I could get."

Across from the post office he noticed a Salvation Army post. That must be where people came from who would be so interested in getting you to heaven they would give you directions and ten cents too. After all, that would buy a cup of coffee and a doughnut. And you could think about heaven better if you weren't hungry.

Continuing his travels, Al found the majority of people who gave him a lift were travelling salesmen, going from one small town to another to pick up orders for hardware or paper goods or bolts of cloth. He had no problem finding places to sleep; outside nearly every city was a tourist camp where he could lay out his blanket. He wrote about the night an ex-soldier called him over and offered him some of his supper—a tasty stew from a Sterno stove—and an army cot. (The ground was hard and pebbly, so the cot was gratefully accepted.) The ex-soldier, learning that Al was heading across the country, jotted down for Al the names of some friends in California who had been in the same regiment.

Every night Al penciled the day's high points in his journal before he went to sleep. He wrote of the group of "gypsies, who gave me the best supper of my trip," roast beef, and hot tea. Then there was the time two "millionaires' sons"—or so they called themselves—gave him some canned cherries and advice on how to "hop a freight."

Anxious to travel a bit faster, Al decided to use their advice. He jotted the results: "I ran for [the freight] but it was going too fast for my load. The caboose tender yelled to me to hurry up but it was futile; I came back. On the siding there was a Barnum and Bailey and Ringling Brothers car." He climbed in, found some men already in there who offered him a drink of ice water. "Asking them how the chances of a job were, I received the answer that they were fine, only the circus was up at Niagara Falls! They were only going that far."

Back on a country road, seeking to hurry his journey, he was offered a lift by a man driving a horse and buggy. Looking back, Al saw a Ford sedan approaching, so turned down the offer from the buggy driver and yes, as he hoped, the sedan stopped and the elderly man invited him to get in. Al did, and began ruing his decision immediately. "For six hours he kept to a careful ten miles an hour," Al wrote, "and expatiated on the evils of twenty-mile-an-hour drivers" while the buggy had long since outdistanced them.

At times Al was dropped off in the wrong town. He lost his mess kit. He was befriended. He was robbed of his blanket. He hopped a freight train that took him a thousand miles out of his way. Still, it was just seventeen days after he started out that he arrived, tired and sore but triumphant, at San Francisco.

Seeing the golden sunset over the Pacific for the first time was a strangely moving experience. As the flaming disk dipped into the water, Al recalled a legend of a mysterious continent out in the Pacific. New emotions rose in him, unfamiliar feelings. His father had gone over that ocean to Hawaii. He recalled Paul's reading Father's letters and the two of them talking of crossing oceans. How he wished for Paul now! Yet in a sense he was traveling for both of them.

As Al began his return trip, he found it increasingly easy to talk to the people he met along the way. It was pleasant to find that others enjoyed hearing his tales, the anecdotes of his trek. A Mr. Kolb, after giving him a lift in his Packard, added an invitation to come home with him for the night. After dinner at the Kolbs', Al sat down at their piano and launched into a series of songs that had the whole family singing.

It was a special satisfaction to know that people would like him for himself, not for the way he fit the image his family had for him since childhood. Yes, he felt he was becoming a man of the world when he spoke offhandedly about the "bulls," and knew the camaraderie of the hoboes. One day, in fact, he found himself stranded in a tiny farming town, then was able to write in his journal that night, "I located the sheriff and obtained the use of the county jail to sleep in." No tender schoolboy, he.

Three months after he had started out, Al was back in Haverford, striding down Berkely Road, picturing Mother's admiring amazement at this stronger, hardier son returning safe from his adventures. Evening had arrived but it was still twilight, neighbors still out chatting over the hedges, though the house lights were on. Not at his house, though. It was dark, it looked empty. He tried the door. It was locked. His aplomb faded.

"Oh, right, you're the young fellow that took off for California," a neighbor spoke up. "No, I don't know where Mrs. Turner is." Another added, "I think she went off in the car with her son."

Using their telephone, Al learned that Mother was indeed at Brinkley's house. He waited as the shadows deepened. Finally Brinkley's Studebaker drove up. Al went out to meet them. Brinkley helped Mother out of the car, then turned to his younger brother. "Well, I see you decided to come back."

As Mother opened her arms, Al embraced her, then turned to Brinkley. "What do you mean, 'decided'? I never said I wasn't coming back. Just because I didn't tell *you* all my plans—"

Mother put her hand on his arm, "Albert, Albert, I'm so glad you're home. We won't argue about anything now."

But Brinkley went on, "You picked a fine time to run off and leave your mother right at a time when she was—we all were—counting on you for a little help. You know the awful loss—you could have been more of a man."

The words stung his new-found confidence. He pushed his face up to his taller brother's. "You don't know what you're talking about!" Mother's firm voice and cool hand separated them. Brinkley drove off with hardly a word.

Apparently the family had the idea that Al had just run away from home, that Paul's death was Mother's loss, their loss, but not *his* loss! And now, when he had tested his manhood in perils, hobo camps and freight trains, when he had made it to the Pacific and back, they called him a child! Worse—"Black sheep." The encounters left him confused and bitter.

If the family did not go out of their way to give the returned wanderer respect and friendship, there were those who did. Al's piano playing was skillful enough to get him occasional stints in local taverns. A regular coterie began to gather, enjoying the music, drinks, and tales of adventure. Al stayed more often with these appreciative friends and less and less at home. He developed a real taste for liquor and other pleasures.

It was around five years before that the Eighteenth Amendment to the Constitution had made "Prohibition" the law of the land, in name at least. But bootleggers and speakeasies were commonplace, an accepted part of society. When they had family dinners, especially at Brinkley's, Al watched as his older brother smilingly brought out the whiskey and Angostura bitters and talked of how good his bootlegger was. So when Al's friends began asking how they could get drinks for a party, Al offered to supply them. "Nothing to it," he assured his admiring friends. But he broke the eleventh commandment—he got caught.

Sitting on the bare mattress of the cot in his cell, Al suffered more at the thought that because he couldn't pay his fine they would call Mother and she would call Brinkley. When the policeman took him out of the cell, gave him back his belt and things, Al hung back. Finally he forced himself to go out where Brinkley stood by the sergeant's desk, folding a receipt. Neither spoke as they walked outside together. Then Al murmured, "Thanks."

Brinkley began quietly, "You're my brother and I love you, but you have caused your family terrible pain. I wonder if you even understand just how much pain your arrest has caused?"

Between clenched teeth Al muttered, "I don't need any lectures."

"You need something you don't have," his brother persisted, "You need the guts to be a man!"

The aggravation of his mother's hurt feelings, his brother's scorn, his sisters' pursed lips, was doubled by Al's inability to get employment, employment that meant anything. Piano playing and tales of travel could take you only so far. He looked at some of the myriad sales "positions" in the *Public Ledger* want ads, but though he tried selling "Realsilk" stockings door to door, and some of the other offers, his heart was never in it.

Following another sales possibility in town on Chestnut Street, Al felt the wind and sun and movement lift his spirits. The bright colors of the recruiting poster caught his eye. U.S. MARINES. The firm chin, the determined face, the sharp uniform. Somehow he found himself whistling, "From the Halls of Montezuma . . ." And the recruiting sergeant smiled. In the back of his mind Al heard the scornful echo, "You need the guts to be a man."

"Eighteen?"

"Sure. Nineteen in October." Al signed the papers with a flourish. Here was more than his answer to Brinkley's challenge. Here was his ticket to the realization of the dreams he had shared with Paul!

He wasn't prepared for Mother's shock when she learned he had enlisted, though she seemed to recover when she told him, "I *am* proud of you, Albert, serving your country—," but then she added, "Of course, I have no idea how I will manage, when you leave, with no man at home."

With his new uniform on, even though he was only five feet ten he felt six feet tall. He said goodbye to his brother Brinkley and the others, smiling proudly. Here was undisputed proof that *he* was fit for the finest service, while Brinkley hadn't even been accepted by the Army when he had tried to enlist in 1917; they turned him down because of his heart. Family and friends wished Al well. Heading for training camp, he thought how great it would be to have all those miles between him and the humiliating hurts at home.

Camp itself was another test, an aching, straining challenge. Drilling until the muscles cried out in pain. Snapping to, at the split second of orders. Taking apart the rifle and putting it back together with precision. Too tired at the day's end to join in card games or other forms of fun.

Then, finally, Cuba! Palms, yes! Hot sand and salty combers on the beaches. After the drills, free time and the girls. Especially Rosita, with the husky laugh and dark eyes and the soft curves that just fit his arms. No Brinkley, no Mother to advise and monitor.

Lying beside Rosita in the evening, he had tried to talk to her about his early dreams, his sharing with Paul, their hopes of some day spanning the world. Now, he had come part way along the journey, but Paul—

"Pablo? Su hermano?" She gave a wiggle and questioning laugh. "Donde está?"

At her question a lump rose in his throat. His tongue felt for the words. "Muerte," Al told her, "He's dead." She smiled and reached for him. He got up and walked away. The wind blew past, rattling the palm leaves, like the click of ghostly fingers. There was a restless, burning yearning creeping through him, a dreadful yearning because he wasn't sure what he was yearning for.

The yearning, unlike fever, didn't pass away; it became a kind of chronic ache. The Cuban rum seemed to help, but the ache returned. After Rosita, Anita—sweet but like down or cotton, soft, accepting, but without understanding.

And there were other trips, other stations—not the Halls of Montezuma, but at least once to the shores of Tripoli. There was this troubling moment: they had been drilling in the sun, then had stopped for a breather. The drab buildings near the beach faded, the uniformed men were no longer there, but music filled the air, a kind of singing chant that brought power and beauty with the sound.

"No-cha, No-cha, A-li-man! No-cha, No-cha, A-li-man!"

He was part of this group of shiny black men, naked ebony muscles, circling, leaping, stepping high and stepping low, following their leader. What a wonderful man! He seemed to radiate love to them all, while the rhythmic chanting filled their minds and hearts—

A sudden slap on the back. The scene shattered.

"Turner! What's the matter? Sun got you?"

As if between two worlds, Al turned foggily. "Did you see them? Dancing?"

"See what? You drunk?"

Al said no more but the strange vision haunted him. It would sometimes return in his dreams, sometimes in a waking memory, but an impossible one. Why would he remember dancing in bare feet to wild harmonies? or racing naked into the surf with hilarious friends? Why the occasional flash of terror as he looked out at the sea? Was this some kind of madness? Yet he could come back to reality in the Corps fast enough, the reality of the sun and the sweat and the work. It was almost as if he had been someone else, here and yet not here.

There were other dreams, other trips, other flashes of ghostly, impossible memories.

Then the hell that was Haiti, and that final incident that blew it. They could not keep him in the Corps, and after that time in the stockade he was glad to get out. He had gone in for pride—he had come out a disgrace. But the others didn't have to know. He *was* an ex-Marine, with an aura of experience, now. With more callouses. And more desires. But no more money.

V
Settling Down

The worst of it was that Mother knew, somehow, about Haiti. How she found out was not so important as the fact that she held this information like a trump card in her hand. Al was her son, her baby, whatever she called him. Mother told him she would help him plan his future and that was that. He had to accept it.

The $400 in pennies was still safe in the lacquer box. Mother now agreed to give it to him, not for college but for a job he could manage. After all, he liked the out-of-doors, he liked meeting people and talking with them, so why not buy a vegetable truck and scales and go from house to house?

There were bright days when the women were glad to come out to his truck and look over the red apples and green lettuce and yellow corn and onions, and Al enjoyed the people and the conversations. Then there were the rainy and windy ones when the side curtains flapped out and the produce got soaked and blown about and he didn't have enough money to buy the next week's supply. Even his brother and sisters buying from him for their growing families didn't gave him enough income to cover his outgo. He kept trying but it was a losing proposition.

Continuing her plans, Mother arranged for Albert to meet a nice girl from a good Main Line family, black-eyed vivacious Martha Nash. Unlike some young women who had found Al exciting as a Marine but dull as a "vegetable man," Martha seemed to find him fascinating. Al liked her whole family, particularly her brothers: he found an almost instant rapport with them. Mother pointed out to him that Martha not only had the kind of beauty Rubens featured, but also was kind and attentive to older people *and* had a good job as a secretary; she would make some man very lucky. Al agreed with her.

In December 1927 Al and Martha were married at St. Luke's Methodist Episcopal Church in Bryn Mawr. Mother made no secret of her delight and her hopes that this was the beginning of the second Albert E. Turner family.

Although Al's skill in talking with people was evident, since he was quickly the center of animated conversations—whether by his truck or with friends or neighbors—it didn't do much for profits from vegetables. However, his brother Brinkley was now doing very well in the investment banking field with his father's firm, Harper and Turner; stock prices were soaring, and here was a field where communicating, getting along well with others, was a real asset. Al left the vegetable business and entered investments.

He had actually liked handling the vegetables; he had a fondness for all growing things. Even the places he'd worked in the garden became beauty spots. But there was something about his being a vegetable man that rubbed his brother and sisters the wrong way. When he had visited around, playing piano and trying to share conviviality, he sensed that Billie and Brinkley, Dot and August or Nan and Paul had an attitude towards him something like the Lysol smell in the bathroom. Now Al began to flourish among the stocks and bonds, where his quick mind, good memory and head for figures backed up his cordiality. This delighted the family, especially Mother. And who ever heard of a black sheep in a gray flannel suit?

The lighthearted lives of "Albie de Kalbie" and "Marbie de Karbie," in their Wynnewood apartment, stayed on Cloud Nine—until that fateful Tuesday, the 29th of October 1929. It was small comfort that everyone else was plunged into the same straits. Day after day, month after month, there were brief pools of income between the arid stretches of unemployment, of scratching, scrimping, scrabbling, borrowing. This stress did not keep Al and Martha from their regular and frequent visits with Mother. Martha would bring books, read to Mother, talk with her about relatives and news; Al offered his affectionate effort, driving Mother around, running errands, helping every way he could think of. Mother used some of this time to travel, to visit Ruth, who had married Gerald Gross and lived in Chevy Chase, Maryland.

Meantime, her older sister, Amelia, who lived in Arden, Delaware had a stroke. Al went to be with her and was there when she died. He stayed to help with arrangements but wrote:

April 26, 1933

Dearest Mother,

    Aunt Amelia's passing has touched my heart; doubly so because of your love for her and your loss. If I can but know that I have done just a little for you by going to see her, then am I satisfied.

Fear, constant fear for her sake and for yours.

Her life was sweet. The good she did lives after her. The memories of her will be only of a marvelous, unselfish, Christlike life.

Dearest Mother, my thoughts and sympathy are with you. Know that it was for the best. If she had gotten better, her life would have been hard. Possibly complete blindness and partial paralysis. God moves in a mysterious way.

It would seem that your life is nothing but bearing burdens. My life is at your command. I want to help you bear your burdens. I love you, dearest Mother o' mine.

I phoned Florence, Mabel, Brink and Dot . . . Rest assured that everything is being done as she would have wished it.

Her life lives after her: record of good deeds.

Any instructions you might want me to carry out, telegraph me collect.

Lovingly,

Albert

Al had truly seemed to revere his mother, often assuring her, "I want to help you bear your burdens." He visited her regularly whenever she was near, though lately she had begun travelling to St. Petersburg, Florida, and to Canada to a Dr. Locke foot clinic, since her arthritis was becoming more and more a handicap. The house on Berkely Road was sold, and when Mother was not in Florida or Canada she stayed occasionally with Nan and Paul, not with Dot and August who simply had no room in their little Lansdowne house (besides, Dot had had a small stroke with partial paralysis of her face). Of course Mother could not live with Al and Martha because their apartment was small and they both worked. Most of the time she stayed with Brink and Billie. After Billie had a nervous breakdown, Mother went to a nursing home.

Wherever Mother stayed, Al and Martha visited her often; sometimes Martha came alone or with some of the Nash family. It seemed as if Al and Martha held Mother as the third in their triad. One book Al gave her as a gift was inscribed, "From your baby, Albert."

But filial affection was no substitute for adequate income in their marriage. Aches and pains of the depression left psychological depression as well. It was in 1935 that Al's sister Dot died, leaving more grief for the families to deal with. Al tried to fight depression, looking for diversion wherever he could find it, which was not in the apartment with Martha, who lashed him verbally for not coming up with the money for their rent and their needs. He tried but sometimes failed. The marriage was shaky. They, even Mother, wondered if a baby might be the answer. Martha had a weight problem; Al had occasional chest pains and indigestion that wasn't indigestion. Still, perhaps—Finally, Martha was pregnant. The baby, little Martha, was born June 3, 1936. She died June 6. Martha went into a deep depression. Al was hospitalized for stomach problems.

While Martha was receiving long-term care from the physician, Al tried to cope with his mounting difficulties in three ways:

—First, by redoubling his efforts with investments. (This had little effect since people were still suspicious of stocks.)

—Second, by delving deep and often into various philosophies he hoped would have clues to the true whereabouts and nature of God. (He found some comfort in the Buddha's advice that release from love of self would bring lessening of sorrow. He tried to explain this to still-grieving Martha, but it only upset her more).

—Third, the quickest painkiller, by drinking with friends.

Though both of them made stabs at trying to create a family life in their apartmenthouse community—Al using his horticulture skills on the roses in the apartment gardens and playing piano at various parties, Martha and Al hosting parties of their own, inviting niece Elaine to play the accordion while the drinks flowed around—it became increasingly obvious these attempts weren't working.

On March 10 1937, Al was rushed to Bryn Mawr Hospital with a heart attack. Dr. Kohlas told Al, as he lay under the oxygen tent, that he had perhaps one more year to live. One more year. Somehow, instead of depressing him, this news seemed to inject Al with a feverish determination to intensify his search through philosophies. He wanted to find out about the nature of God while he was still in *this* life! He *had to* become spiritually aware! This became more important than anything else, marriage, job, anything he would leave behind when he died. Al read more, read faster, hoping to find clues to the spiritual path.

In the *Bhagavad-Gita* he found that "Work done with anxiety about results is far inferior to work done without such anxiety, in the calm of self-surrender. Seek refuge in the knowledge of Brahman. They who work selfishly for results are miserable." Perhaps this had helped make his past miserable, this anxiety about results, income, commissions, rent, bills. Al resolved not to be anxious any more.

He could surrender himself and still help others without being anxious. Almost every other day he helped Mother in some way, typing letters for her, running errands, taking her on one of her many tours of cemeteries—for she had to visit not only West Laurel Hill but also the place where Dot was buried and Wayne, where baby Martha lay. In early November he drove Mother to Washington to visit Ruth, who was having problems with her son, her twin girls and her marriage.

This left it to Martha to come up with the rent. Again. She sent Brinkley a special delivery letter asking if he could lend her the money, venting her angry frustrations that Al had "threatened to go on a drunk" if she went to her family instead of his. Brinkley came up with the rent.

The months came and went. March 10, 1938 dawned, the date the doctor had felt might be his last—and Al did not die. He had, indeed, felt a bit more prepared for the end, if it were near, because he had been working on the search, on self-surrender, on spiritual study, and he had cut down on his drinking. Whichever the reason, Al was now able to go back into investments—though of course on commission only, which meant "No sales, no income." But there were some sales, then more sales, and Al took up a study of railroad bonds and finances to become more of a specialist and better able to help clients with their portfolios. Railroads, after all, were just about the steadiest, surest segment of the market.

Albert E. Turner Jr. began leading three lives: one, as the manager of the Trading Department of Auchincloss, Parker and Redpath, using his financial skills; the second, as Martha's husband, keeping up the apartment, visiting his family and hers, of whom he was increasingly fond; the third, as a man involved in study and service. Al regularly led a Sunday School class at St. Luke's Methodist Church; he worked with the YMCA and with the Red Cross, teaching life-saving and other classes. He kept adding to his collection of books, particularly Rosicrucian literature, delving farther for clues into the mystery of the Immortal. Martha, on the other hand, preferred the tangible, pay checks and paid bills; life was hard enough without trying to look into some strange Never-Never Land.

VI
A Way Out

Martha's health was fragile. Al's however, seemed improving. In fact, his mother's diary noted that "Al gave a transfusion for Martha" in June and July of 1938, three months after his own predicted demise. Al credited his philosophical studies with increasing his life and his growing religious activity as well.

In 1939, as the fighting in Europe heated up and defense industries in the United States rumbled into high gear, Al gave increasing time to volunteer work for the Red Cross. He wondered, too, if there was something more that the St. Luke's Church Bible Class could be doing in these tense times.

Meanwhile, he and Martha had moved to a better apartment in Wynnewood in the spring of 1940. With Brinkley's help, Mother was moved from the nursing home in Ambler, where she complained that the nurses were inconsiderate and one had even stolen something from her room, to a home called The Oaks, in Wyncote, where the staff and guests seemed more considerate. There she continued as a matriarch as best she could, received regular visits from most of her children and many grandchildren, and was dismayed to learn her daughter Anna was getting divorced. She hoped nothing like that would happen with Al and Martha.

In January of 1941, Al had his second heart attack. Surprisingly he was out of the hospital more quickly than the first time. He seemed to gain strength from throwing his energies into service in church activities and Red Cross training, now teaching adult classes in first aid for civil defense.

He spent less time at home; there was less and less to share there—until the tragedy of the death of Stanley Nash, Martha's brother and his dear friend, in 1945. Grief was shared, but not closeness. The closeness was rather with the men of the Bible Class, with Stanley's four brothers, Frank, who was class president, Thomas, Harvey and James, and the other servicemen who were putting their religion into more than words.

"The Servicemen's Bible Class" grew rapidly to one of the favorites of the Main Line area. Its soldiers, sailors and airmen were dubbed the "St. Luke's Angels" and received accolades from the local press. Besides winning sport championships in competitions, with Al's encouragement the "St. Luke's Angels" arranged to give many volunteer hours helping the patients and nurses at Bryn Mawr Hospital. (One nurse, Mildred Hanck, found volunteer Dick Eckenroth such an "angel" she became his wife.)

Meanwhile Al was getting more phone calls, not so much for unpaid bills as for speaking engagements. The Red Cross featured him on its Speaker's Bureau:

ALBERT EDWARD TURNER, JR.

Mr. Turner has participated in almost every phase of Red Cross work. He has served as a Certified Red Cross Instructor for First Aid and Accident Prevention, and has been working for the Camp and Hospital Council, Disaster Preparedness and Relief Committee, and the (1946 recently discontinued) Prisoner of War Packaging Center. His zealous recruitment of Volunteer Nurses' Aides, Blood Donors, Home Nursing Classes and Surgical Dressing classes contributed greatly to the achievements of these groups. He has served with the U.S. Marine Corps, is a member of the Board of Directors of the Investment Corporation of Philadelphia, and is an analyst for the brokerage firm of Auchincloss, Parker and Redpath.

Returning from one speaking engagement still warmed by the audience applause and the thanks of the program chairman, Al felt as if he had slipped back in time and could feel his father's hand on his shoulder, Father's special words, "Well done, Al boy!"

He opened the apartment door.

"You're late. You said you'd be here half an hour ago! There's the mail—some new bills, some overdue bills and a letter from the Red Cross."

Opening the Red Cross letter, Al read aloud, "You have served as a volunteer Safety Service Instructor for a period of over five years. In recognition of this splendid record, a Continuous Service bar, issued by our Volunteer Special Services, will be presented to you at the Annual Banquet . . ."

Martha's acid comment: "Oh, sure. They'll give you a little pin and tell you what a good boy you were. Too bad they never give you anything you can pay a bill with!"

What could he answer? Her comments kept coming: he wasn't making enough money, they were barely scraping by while he spent time on things that didn't amount to a red cent. Not only that, she was sure he was playing around with those nurses' aides he was recruiting. To make it worse he was poisoning his mind with those strange books he was reading. They ought to be burned! At least they'd be good for warming up the apartment!

Al tried yelling back but that only made things worse. He could walk out and shut the door behind him—and he did.

It was as if he was in a tunnel, a long tunnel with a noisy train coming closer and closer behind him, but he couldn't find the way out. There had to be an exit, a way out, somewhere. Phrases he had memorized in high school as a kind of memorial to Father, phrases from the Sermon on the Mount, kept coming back to mind.

"Blessed are the poor in spirit, . . .

"Blessed are they that mourn, . . .

"Blessed are the meek, . . ."

He tried concentrating on the Beatitudes each day as he worked in the office and as he prepared his Sunday Bible classes.

A third heart attack put him back in Bryn Mawr Hospital. Many of his Bible Class students came in to visit and tell him they needed him. In near record time he was back on his feet. Was it because of the Sermon on the Mount? There were so many insights in those verses in Matthew. Perhaps part of his service should be to share these more widely.

On Laymen's Sunday, a cold February 22nd in 1948, St. Luke's Methodist Episcopal Church in Bryn Mawr had advertised widely that:

THE SERMON ON THE MOUNT

The greatest sermon ever given anywhere
will be quoted from memory by
a Main Line Businessman.
See how this sermon can help you in YOUR
everyday business life.

The church program listed:

MESSAGE "The Exposition of the Sermon on the Mount"
Albert E. Turner, Jr., "Main Line business man."

As Al stepped to the pulpit, he felt a tightness in his chest, his palms were moist. Then he saw in the front pews the men from his Bible class, grinning encouragement.

As he began to talk, it was almost as if he were standing by the crowd on the hill nearly 2,000 years ago, sharing a personal experience.

Afterwards, men and women of the congregation crowded around him. "Great, Albert!" "Thank you, Mr. Turner!" "Would you please, Mr. Turner . . ." brought echoes of other memories.

For a moment the thought came that when his father had received such comments a generation ago, his mother and in fact the whole Turner family had been at the church supporting him. But for him, Albert Junior, not his mother nor his brothers or sisters or wife were there (Martha was feeling ill again). Just friends. But what friends!

Still, it came time to say goodbye, leave the warm church and go out in the cold, back to the apartment where he had to take the role of Black Sheep of the Turner Family. It was laid out day after day in so many of Martha's questions. Why didn't he spend more time with her? Why didn't he do better at his job, why couldn't they afford more? Why did he read those crazy books? Al tried to insulate himself from the questions by delving even deeper into the books, into ancient teachings—the Egyptians, Zoroaster, the Greeks, Indian sages, opening doors into another world where what mattered was Love and God and the Spirit of God in Man. As for the rent and other bills, "Take no thought for the things of the morrow . . ." "Be not anxious for results . . ." The greatest thinkers seemed to agree clearly on this: Money was not meant to be important. The goals of life were not those reached by so many thousand dollars, but those reached by inner discipline, by character, mental and spiritual stretching and straining, rather than physical sweat or commercial calculation.

The Rosicrucians, he read, were a group of great men who possessed inner power, who knew the secret of the mastery of life. They included such men as Francis Bacon, Issac Newton, and Benjamin Franklin. One of the abilities developed by the Rosicrucians was that of expelling unwanted thoughts. How great it would be for him to just expel the ugly bitterness that kept rising like a backed-up drain when he was accused of failing his obligations! He drew courage from reading of candidates for the Order with "heads bowed in grief, burdened with personal problems, cynical and bitter," who crossed the thresholds of the ancient mystical temples and emerged "inspired, confident, self-reliant." He joined.

Men who rocked the world had touched a source of confidence and inspiration. Socrates, Zoroaster, Buddha, Confucius, Jesus Christ, all had had visions. All had been troubled, had retreated from the world for a time—forty days in the wilderness or fourteen days under the Bo tree, each in his own way—and had returned filled with enlightenment.

Al finally found a place of tranquility, not in the wilderness or under the Bo tree, but at a Quaker haven for study and meditation in Wallingford: Pendle Hill. There Al found Howard Brinton, a Friend and philosopher, with whom he could talk about his searching. Brinton seemed to have within himself a sense of personal peace. Al could speak with him about the *Bhagavad-Gita,* of the Atman, the Godhead that is within every being; Brinton could give insights on the ancient texts as well as modern philosophies. He reminded Al that the Society of Friends held the belief that there was "that of God" in every man; that each man could bring about peace—but it had to begin within the Self before it could reach others. Al treasured the time he spent with Brinton.

Closer to home, Al was surprised and glad to find that Billie's mother, Mrs. W. J. Savage, was another one who was both interested and eager to discuss religious philosophies. "Muddie," as Billie called her, had come from her Louisiana home to stay with her daughter and son-in-law—creating some tensions with Brinkley, who was somewhat bitter that his own mother was in a nursing home while "Muddie" was their guest. "Muddie" Savage was well versed not only in the literature of the Rosicrucians, of which she had several books, but also in the works of the savant, Krishnamurti. She shared with Al her books and a manuscript she had written. Though her face had an odd expression, because of one eyelid's permanent droop as a result of an illness, her voice was dry and calm as she talked with Al of "the divine intuitive principle which needs no book, but lives always in the presence of the Absolute Intelligence. Surely, if our Christian Bible teaches us anything, it is this, that 'we are *one* with Him,' and 'When He shall appear we shall be like Him!'"

Trying to grasp the reins of these forces which seemed to be pulling his life in different directions, Al found the very idea of being "one with Christ" awesome, not really comprehensible, almost frightening. He felt a desperate pressure building within him, a pressure to get away into his own "wilderness," to find his own "Bo tree." And yet he could not really get away from the activities of business, family and church. This was 1949, not 1924 when he had simply dropped everything and hitchhiked west. And even then he had returned not to happiness but to distress. Would it ever be possible for him to find that inner peace, that enlightenment that he so thirsted for? Or would it stay a shimmering mirage?

Then a friend from church said, "I found a book I think you'll be interested in," and handed him a copy of Thomas Sugrue's *There Is A River,* "The Story of Edgar Cayce." Al accepted the book with polite thanks, read the first few pages incredulously, then began to devour the rest of it like a starved man. He carried it everywhere with him. (He would not leave it at home, for a couple of his favorite books had disappeared and he guessed that Martha had considered them unhealthy and disposed of them.) As Al read how Edgar Cayce, an ordinary man, a meek man caught up in most extraordinary circumstances, had become a channel for God's help for other, he felt like a man lost at sea who had suddenly found a compass.

When he reached the part of the book that told how to join the Association of Research and Enlightenment, which Cayce had founded, he wrote out a check for membership in the ARE and mailed it without a word to Martha. From that time, with each piece of mail from the ARE, whether *Searchlight* bulletins, extracts from the Cayce readings, or results of follow-up studies on some of the work done since Cayce's death in 1945, Al's hope was renewed.

It seemed that miracles were possible now, through healing information in the "readings" given by the psychic in a trance some years ago. Al had a friend, a young man whose life was slowly being drained by multiple sclerosis, for which they knew no cure. Surely, in the thousands of readings he gave, Edgar Cayce must have said something to help heal sufferers from MS. Excitedly, Al wrote for help.

VII
A Need For Healing

While Albert lay in enforced quiet in his hospital bed, Gladys had the opposite problem: —each day so filled with activities that, except for the brief noontime meditation for the ARE staff, there was scarcely a moment for reflection. Not until she had finished her day's work and her evening hospital visit, had returned home and caught up with urgent correspondence and phone calls and had watered her plants . . . not until then could she stretch out and relax.

It was easy then to recall that summer day in 1949 when the letter from the worried man in Philadelphia had arrived in the pile of mail for the A.R.E. secretary. Gladys had scanned it quickly:

> I have read about Edgar Cayce in *There is a River* by Thomas Sugrue, and have sent in my dues for membership in the A.R.E. Now I need any information you can send me on the disease of multiple sclerosis. A young friend of mine seems to be suffering severely from it.
> Blessings for your help.
>
> Albert E. Turner

Since she had first come to work for Edgar Cayce in 1923, Gladys had had a warm, almost filial relationship with the man people called "The Sleeping Prophet." She had sat beside him with her notebook as he put himself into a sleeping trance. After he began speaking in answer to questions (usually put to him by Mrs. Cayce) she would write down what he said for those who had requested help for their illnesses or other problems, even when they were hundreds of miles away. Thus she had taken down most of the 14,156 trance sessions or "readings" that had made him America's best-documented psychic. In the four years since his death in 1945, even though she had spent most of her time compiling and indexing information from the readings, she and the staff working with her had barely made a dent in the 49,135 pages of verbatim material.

Still, there was often enough clear and accessible material to answer requests like this. She checked the index. Yes, some readings had given information on treatment for multiple sclerosis. Medical information, of course, was sent only to members; still, this inquirer appeared to qualify. She mailed him a few excerpts that she had compiled from readings on MS patients, including a reading which a doctor had obtained on the disease itself.

A brief note came back quickly: "Thank you for the material. Now I am trying to find a doctor who is willing to use the treatments suggested in the readings."

The flow of requests for information from all over the country kept the staff busy.

In November, these terse lines from Albert Turner:

> "Unable to find any doctor who would give treatments. My friend died yesterday."

What could they tell him? Although the A.R.E. had names of some doctors willing to give treatments prescribed in the Cayce readings, there were none in his area. The files held many similar heartbreaks. This type of reluctance had been evident ever since Edgar Cayce first diagnosed his own throat problem years ago in Hopkinsville, Kentucky. Eventually there had been some physicians who had the courage to try the advice given by these trance readings, and those who did (especially Wesley Ketchum) often surprised themselves at the successes. But most doctors simply would not risk trying anything which had not been AMA approved.

In December, another type of letter came to the top of Gladys's mail pile. This one asked for information from the Edgar Cayce readings on the Bible, particularly, the *Book of Revelation*. "I plan to use this material," the letter continued, "in teaching my interdenominational Sunday School class in St. Luke's Methodist Church in Bryn Mawr. —Albert E. Turner"

As Gladys put some of the readings' mimeographed *Revelation* material into an envelope, her first feeling was, *How in the world does he have the nerve?* The Edgar Cayce materials on the *Book of Revelation* were so far removed from any traditional church teachings, so different from any Sunday School teaching mterial she had ever heard of—*How could he think to teach with such material?* This Mr. Turner had never taken part in one of the A.R.E. Study Groups, had never studied under Mr. Cayce, had not even *known* him.

Gladys held a feeling of respect akin to awe for the source of the readings. So many thousands of times she had sat near Edgar Cayce's side as he lay back on the couch in his study, had clasped his hands over his solar plexus and had begun the breathing that led to the trance-like state. Gladys had heard this eighth-grade graduate use complex medical terminology in his answers, had heard his voice give information on people, places and events which the man, Edgar Cayce had no way of knowing.

There was a steady flow of work through her office in the old Cayce home on Arctic Crescent, which then served as A.R.E. Headquarters: extracting, compiling, indexing; weekly newsletters and readings extracts, plus a monthly bulletin; there was also correspondence with the members, answering inquiries, some with form replies, others with individual information.

"January 19, 1950"

Gladys typed the date on another letter. Would she ever get through the stack of papers on her desk? A knock on the door. Another interruption! This time the membership secretary had brought a man to her office.

"This new member seems to want more information than he has already received, and asked if you might help him—Mr. Albert Turner."

Gladys looked up, her smile polite.

A D'Artagnan in a well-traveled business suit, the man gave a courtly bow.

She recalled the name; her eyes were wary. "Oh, yes—Mr. Turner, the man who teaches *Revelation* in his Sunday School class!"

He broke into a delighted laugh. "You remembered!"

Gladys tried to maintain her calm while this man kept his brown eyes on her as if he could not look away.

She drew a deep breath, then demanded, "How do you get away with it? This is anything but traditional information!"

He just stood there, smiling.

Finally she found herself mirroring his smile. She prompted, "You had a question?"

He suddenly came alert. "Oh, yes. I had a question, but it's not as important as the one I'm about to ask. May I take you to lunch?"

At the Golden Dragon Restaurant, as they spoke of the readings and *Revelation,* Gladys wondered why he seemed so different from the hundreds of others who had come to inquire about the readings.

Albert Turner radiated intensity when he spoke of his search, of his elation on discovering James Pryse's book, *The Apocalypse Un-*

sealed, where he found the *Book of Revelation* described as "a manual of spiritual development and not, as conventionally interpreted, a cryptic history or prophecy." A portion of the Cayce reading #281–16 seemed to have more than a clue to this, indeed a key to better understanding:

> "Why, then, ye ask now, was this written (this version) in such a manner that is hard to be interpreted, save in the experience of every soul who seeks to know, to walk in a closer communion with Him? . . . For the visions, the experiences, the names, the churches, the places, the dragons, the cities, all are but emblems of those forces that may war within the individual in its journey . . ."

Does this mean," Albert Turner had asked, "that the words of *Revelation* have to be understood as emblems or symbols and then actually experienced by the one who wants to know their real meaning?"

Then somehow they were talking about the readings, about Mr. Cayce, about their backgrounds, about life, about God.

Gladys was able to give him additional material to take back to Philadelphia, but he kept returning more and more frequently.

He was there when Gladys's little house was finished on her lot next to the former Cayce home, and the words "W E L C O M E T O   G L A D   N I C H E" inscribed on the new cement sidewalk.

He was there when the sink trap had to be removed; he was there when the screen door warped and wouldn't close. Almost every weekend he was there, bringing a plant, a flower, a gardenia bush.

"You mustn't bring me so many flowers," Gladys protested, "or I'll have to get a greenhouse to take care of them all!"

"That's a wonderful idea!" Al's genial face lit up. "Some day I'll put one right here in your front yard."

She shook her head, laughing. "I didn't mean that!"

But there were many quiet moments.

Peace of mind and peace of heart—Al had been searching for it all his life, he told her, all across the country. Now, he knew, he felt closer to it in Virginia Beach.

VIII
On a Wing and a Prayer

To Al, Virginia Beach was an oasis of peace, but the more he returned there the worse the atmosphere in his Wynnewood apartment.

The bitter tensions culminated in another heart attack, Al's fourth. In Bryn Mawr Hospital, again under the oxygen tent, he recalled with a sense of irony how Dr. Kohlas had given him one year to live after his 1937 attack. Yet here he was with the imcapacity, the pain, thirteen years later.

Dear God, he thought, *What are You trying to tell me?* It was hard, when so many inner voices were talking in his mind, to know just which might be God's. If only there could be some kind of fine tuning of the mind that could pick out God's voice, could make it clearer. Maybe there was. If only he could find it!

Weakly he reached for the book which he had insisted on keeping with him even on the trip to the hospital, *There Is A River*. He leafed through the pages, finally reaching the chapter on philosophy. His fingers tightened as his eyes lit on these words in the archaic phrasing used by the entranced Cayce:

> Each soul enters the material plane not by chance, but through the grace, the mercy, of a loving Father; that the soul may, through its own choice, work out those faults, those fancies, which prevent the communion and at-onement with the Creative Forces. . . .
>
> As ye do unto the least of thy brethren, so ye do it unto thy Maker. These are laws . . .

The source which spoke through the seer seemed to be saying that there was indeed a purpose even for this heart attack, a purpose for what he—for what everyone—had to endure in living, to correct something that was preventing "at-onement."

"At-onement" was so much like *atonement,* making up for something sinful, but it was different, it called for being "one" with the

Christ-consciousness, a concept that was close but not quite within his reach.

There was so much here, so many answers for questions he was only beginning to form, questions which somehow had a faintly familiar ring to them as if he might have asked them ages ago, but he knew he hadn't—in this life.

Gradually his heart beat with more regularity. His circulation improved; his blood pressure neared normal. The day came when the doctors told him he could go home, sooner than they had first hoped.

Back home in the apartment, Martha was both anxious and angry. How were they going to manage? He better not think of ever going to Virginia Beach again. How much did they owe his doctor, her doctor? How soon would he go back to work? He better put those crazy books away. Couldn't he see what a strain she had been under?

Al felt the need to empty his mind and heart of the strident worries. He sat in the meditating lotus posture, eyes closed, palms open, and intoned the ancient chant, not just "OM" but a long, drawn-out "AHHHH—UUUUU—MMMMM . . ."

Martha's shriek of frustration: "I can't *stand* it!"

Al drew a deep breath and slowly stood up. "All right. You won't have to. I'll leave."

He moved into an apartment in Philadelphia.

His mother, totally crippled by arthritis, died in the Wyncote nursing home in March of 1951.

Divorce proceedings began.

Time passed in two speeds: weekends flew by, in Virginia Beach; weekdays crawled, in Philadelphia.

Christmas Eve.

The DC-4 from Philadelphia circled the Norfolk airport once, again and then again. Passengers peered eagerly through the windows, but not even airport lights were visible through the fog. Seatbelts were tight for landing; nerves were tighter. Wives whose husbands were waiting down below, husbands whose wives had driven to the airport with the children in the car, anxious to pick up Daddy and get home to finish trimming the tree and hanging the stockings.

A portly man glanced at his watch and muttered to his companion,

"I promised Sarah that if the kids were in bed by now I'd assemble the bicycle."

A tot in a pink snow-suit pulled her mother's sleeve. "When will we get there, Mommy?" When her mother responded with, "Shut up!" she began to cry. Mother patted her. Whispers grew raspy.

The captain's voice came over the speaker: "Due to fog conditions, we are unable to land at Norfolk Airport. We are proceeding to Richmond . . ." The rest of what he said did not make much difference. It was Christmas Eve. And the waiting families below would have waited in vain. It was a long way back from Richmond by car—two hours at least *without* the fog. The calm assurance of the planned flight was cracked.

"Damn!" said the young man with the curly beard.

"Richmond? But I don't *know* anybody in Richmond!" The white-haired lady expostulated.

The stout man with the brief case had begun to sweat, though it wasn't warm. The eleven-year-old boy beside him had his eyes squeezed tight shut, thought his lips were moving.

The stewardesses were talking reassuringly, moving calmly through the aisle, but tensions stayed high as the plane droned through the bleak nothingness.

"How long will our fuel hold out?"

"Dear God, I want to go *home* on Christmas Eve!" The mother's voice was on the edge of tears.

The man with the rumpled brown hair looked around him at the strained faces, the tense young woman twisting her engagement ring, the stout grandmother whose chin was beginning to tremble, the perspiring man, the boy with his tight shut eyes.

"Elaine," the man called to the stewardess, "I just happen to have something here . . ." He reached overhead and lifted down a small guitar.

The stewardess's face lit up. "Oh, Al, that's great. I didn't know you could play the guitar."

"I don't," he answered with a grin, "I just play at it. And here is something else." He reached into his luggage and brought out a bottle. "A bit of medicine for some passengers with bad nerves." As the stewardess then passed drinks to the passengers who wanted them, he began to strum the guitar.

The unexpected chords quieted the fretful queries. The praying boy opened his eyes, saw the middle-aged businessman really did have a guitar in his lap.

"Happy birthday, everybody!" Al laughed.

"Don't you mean 'Merry Christmas'?" the boy asked, smiling now, "You just goofed!"

"Birthday too," the musician insisted, his own grin beginning to be reflected in the other faces. "Every day is a new day—and we have a new life for that new day! Every day we can be born again! And Christmas was a very special birthday, back in Bethlehem." Then he asked the boy, "How often can you be up where Santa's sleigh goes, on Christmas Eve?"

Now the passengers were looking at him as if he had suddenly sprouted a full white beard and carried a pack of toys on his back.

"This just has to be a time for joy," he continued, "'Joy to the World!' I can't play so well, but if you'll sing real loud, nobody'll notice." He struck a chord, and as his voice rang out, first the children and then the other passengers joined in. By ones and twos they got out of their seats and crowded around this man who had magically become a troubador.

"It Came Upon A Midnight Clear," they sang, and childish voices joined the grownups with "Away In A Manger."

In the cockpit, however, the captain was sputtering words quite different as he struggled to right the now tilting DC-4. But he, as the stewardesses, knew Al Turner as that friendly but peculiar passenger who often flew between Philadelphia and Norfolk, who greeted them each time he got on the plane with "Happy Birthday!" At a time like this, it was easier for the captain to level the plane than to calm a load of frightened passengers as they headed from the Chesapeake fog towards distant Richmond.

All the way, the cabin rang. As voices lifted in carols, spirits lifted. After the plane landed, the passengers spoke their thanks as they got off. As the last ones stepped down, Stewardess Elaine VanNoy reached for Al's hand. "You gave so much love to everyone!"

"It was there all the time, Elaine," Al assured her. "It was fun to help bring it out. I feel so much of it myself, when I'm with Gladys."

The captain laid a hand on Al's shoulder. "If that's what makes you so cheerful, keep on seeing her."

Al's smile glowed: "I will."

Twenty years later, Elaine VanNoy Ollio, who was stewardess on that plane, wrote to Gladys after learning that Gladys Davis Turner was coming to her town, Miami, to speak about the A.R.E.

February 10, 1972

Dear Mrs. Turner,

I was so delighted to hear that you were coming to Miami. I heard about you almost twenty years ago to the date . . . . Al Turner . . . had introduced me to Edgar Cayce Readings and the studies, etc., when I was a stewardess flying from Newark to Norfolk, and Al used to get on at Philadelphia, and somehow or other he took to my roommate, Shirley, and I as his favorite crew. . . . (Of course he was also a favorite of ours, as he always had a ray of light or sunshine to give everyone.)

To be honest with you, Mrs. Turner, when he first flew with us, we thought him a little "different," that he was so giving . . .

One Christmas Eve Al got on our flight and had a guitar and we were headed for Norfolk. When we got over the airport, it was fogged in and we circled for quite a while, and found out we could not land. There were many wives waiting in Norfolk, many husbands on board, on Christmas Eve—What a disappointment! So Al brought out his guitar and also a bottle of some kind of liquor and we (illegally) served the passengers upon Al's request. He played the guitar, as we had our Captain call Virginia and explain our not landing.

Al soothed all the people and they crowded around him as he played Christmas songs on his guitar—not to the delight of the captain. At the time, the weight and balance of a DC-4 was more important than now with big jets, but the Captain, Shirley and the crew loved Al and trimmed up for it. . . . Anyway, Al soothed all aboard and he gave so much love to everyone. You must have been proud to have been his wife. He told me how much he loved you before he was even married to you—so I really would love to meet you. . . .

Hoping and looking forward to meeting you,

Sincerely,

Elaine VanNoy Ollio

IX
Many Lifetimes

There was no doubt in Al's mind that he would keep on seeing Gladys, or that he would eventually make the center of his life Virginia Beach. That compulsive search was steering him there, the search that included the child wanting to know the whereabouts of God, the young man seeking his own identity, the struggling man trying to find solutions in philosophies. Sometimes he felt like a desert camel heading for the oasis that was the A.R.E. Headquarters, with its thousands of readings of Edgar Cayce, with its shelves of great ideas and great lives, philosophers and prophets and pragmatic scientists. And the cheerful help from such fine people. And above all, Gladys!

How anybody could know as much as she did, carry on as many activities, be so beautiful, yet so centered in faith! It was his constant wonder.

But there were many problems in the way of transition. He was working for a Philadelphia firm with Philadelphia clients, some of whom were personal friends. There was no way he could continue with this firm from Virginia Beach. He had no savings to speak of. The divorce was not yet final. All he could manage were occasional weekend trips—and even then he was lucky if he could see Gladys for more than a few brief hours. Her work as secretary for the A.R.E. Board involved her with their Congress and other activities on weekends too.

Al was tied by circumstances, tugged by loneliness.

His family lent nothing in the way of support, not just because of sympathy with Martha. His brother and sisters were struggling in their own whirlpools of distress. Brinkley and Nan were trying to work out the disposition of the little left in Mother's estate after the nursing home was paid; Nan and Paul were breaking up their marriage after four children and a silver anniversary. August was a widower, with his own four children to think about. Ruth, now divorced, was having more than a casual nervous breakdown. So here Al was, the youngest of this family that Albert E. Turner, Sr. had prayed about and aimed towards greatness; here he was—in limbo.

When depression washed over him like a cold, salt wave, Al would pull out a snapshot he had taken of Gladys standing in her little front yard. In the background you could clearly see the statue of the crucified Christ, the statue which was actually in the foreground of the church across the street, the Star of the Sea Roman Catholic Church. (Al and Father Nicholas Habets became good friends, visiting across the road, exchanging jokes and thoughts. Later Father Habets helped build and was the first priest of St. Nicholas Catholic Church on Lynnhaven Road, Virginia Beach.)

One night as Al held the little photo in his hand, he felt a compulsion to as express his feelings—but there was only the ticking clock for company. He picked up his pen and a sheet of paper:

"Across the street from the 'Man on the Cross'
Lives a maiden so fair there is never a loss
From her beauty, so gentle, so kind and so sweet
I could live all my life right there at her feet. . .
All I have is her picture. . ."

It was so hard to find words for the feelings he had for Gladys, but the words were all he had. He stared at the photo. It was so right that the Christ statue should be there, behind her.

"— her queenly mien
'The evidence of things unseen.'"

It had been an exhausting day, but he couldn't stop writing. He searched for rhymes. His pen scratched on for 22 lines, finishing,

"As the night lengthens on, my soul longs for sleep,
In the lonesomeness. Sowing. Shall I ever reap?"

He folded the paper. It was strange how you could be physically all right but hurting so, in other ways. He seemed to be on a treadmill, plodding and dragging and helping the mill to turn. Someone had said "The mills of the gods grind slowly. . ." There had to be a purpose to it all—but what sort of purpose could there be to his life, that so far had been filled with mistakes and mishaps?—His father and his dearest brother dead, his family looking down on him, his attempt to prove himself in the Marines then messing up, his inability to earn much money, his heart attacks, marriage problems, and now—all he had for company, for comfort, was paper. That photo of Gladys, her letter, the day's mail.

He picked up the latest A.R.E. Bulletin. The January, 1952, feature for major study was Reincarnation. They had scheduled several speakers, including a physician from Wilmington, Delaware, who was making a special study of reincarnation by hypnotically regressing subjects to past lives. Al knew he had to attend that lecture.

The idea that he had lived before was easy for him to accept—far easier than the thought that there had been nothing, no spirit of his, *before* his birth. All of his studies pointed to it. In ancient Greece, Pythagoras, the great philosopher-mathematician, had claimed he actually remembered who he had been in his previous life. Many Greeks and Romans had believed the souls in Hades could drink of Lethe, the River of Forgetfulness, then return and be born again in the upper world. Sri Krishna had said that just as worn-out garments were shed by the body, so worn-out bodies were shed by the one who dwells within the body. New bodies were put on like garments, according to the *Bhagavad-Gita*. Hindu belief had included not only rebirth but the effect of Karma—what you deserved from your actions—on your next life; the untouchables were born into that lowest order because of what they had done in the life before. The Theosophists believed, and so did the Rosicrucians.

He leafed again through *There Is A River* to the chapter on philosophy, to Cayce's words

> Life is a purposful experience, and the place in which a person finds himself is one in which he may use his present abilities, faults, failures, virtues, in fulfilling the purpose for which the soul decided to manifest in the three-dimensional plane.

This went beyond those others. Souls were not born *by accident*; they "decided" to manifest or be born, for a *purpose*. Even their faults and failures could be used!

So there *had* to be a purpose for his life, a purpose that could make use of his many faults and failures! If there was a way to look at the previous lives, there could be a way to find that purpose.

Sitting with the audience in the A.R.E. auditorium, Al listened with appreciation as the Wilmington physician began his talk. Dr. Henry George was not only well versed in his subject, he was confident. He gave some historical background then asked the audience who among them had at some time met a stranger and instantly felt they had known him before? A surprising number of hands went up. Who among them, coming to a place they had never been before, remembered it—perhaps slightly changed, as it had been in the past? Again, hands were raised. Sometimes we "remember" things we could not have encountered in this life, Dr. George said, yet we do not really understand what memory is. We just accept what it gives us, or reject it as a "dream" when we don't understand it.

Hypnosis was a tool, he said, which could help bring to the foreground parts of our memories that would normally be inaccessible to us. Which of us could now recall, for instance, our fifth birthday party? And yet, under hypnosis, a subject could be taken back in time to that particular day and remember clearly not just the cake and candles but the name of every guest at the party and even the presents they gave! He, himself, had regressed volunteers not just to age five, or age two, or the time of birth, but even farther back—when they had recalled living in a different time, with a different name—back even two or three lifetimes! Dr. George was interested in working with such volunteers in part to find people who remembered living recently enough so details of the past life could be checked.

Al went up to him after the lecture.

"I have reason to believe I have lived before." Al told of the strange, brief flashes of other times and places, such as the blacks dancing on the Tripoli beach, which had come unbidden across his consciousness. "Would you be interested in hypnotizing me to see if we can identify anything?"

"Can you come to my office in Wilmington?"

"Certainly. After all, that's right on the way from Philadelphia to Virginia Beach!"

He thought Gladys would be pleased and excited to learn of the planned regressions, but she was not. She was just concerned.

"Are you sure you want to do this? You know Mr. Cayce said the main reason for learning about previous lives was not for research, but to do better in *this* life."

Al explained he hoped to discover a purpose for what he was going through, then reminded her, "After all, Mr. Cayce gave a reading that told some of *your* previous lives."

"Yes," Gladys admitted, "and it helped me to understand more about the relationships I would have to work with. Of course, Mr. Cayce gave a great many Life Readings—readings that told about former lifetimes—that led people to understand where their problems originated, and sometimes uncovered talents they didn't realize they had."

"Well—"

"But it was Mr. Cayce who put *himself* in a trance. These people whose lives he spoke of were not hypnotized."

"Please don't worry," Al reassured her, "Henry George is an M.D. and a very respected one."

Gladys was still not comfortable with the idea that Al should be hypnotized—not for the length of time such regression sessions would take. Al, on the other hand, was enthusiastic about the possibilities.

Not until May did Dr. George find the time and the witnesses he considered necessary for these sessions.

It was in May, also, that the divorce was granted. This should indeed be a time for a new life. But what kind of life could he build on the foundation of his old life—or was it old *lives*?

On the evening of May 22, 1952 Albert Turner reclined on a couch in the office of Dr. Henry George in Wilmington. Witnesses included Mrs. Henry George, Dr. Marion Dick, Frank Nelson, Esq., and Robert O'Hora, Esq. A wire recorder was turned on. [Detailed material from these transcripts may be found in the Appendix. The original recordings for three sessions also were found, through serendipity; they were played back and transferred to cassettes. From these we were able to hear the tones of voice, of music, and the pronunciation, which in some cases appeared to differ from the transcripts.]

The mild-mannered, brown-haired doctor quickly had Al in a deep trance. Gradually Al was regressed to the age of two.

Al: . . . Somebody spilled something on me.
Dr: Where were you?
Al: 6366 Wodbine Avenue
Dr: When? What year?
Al: 1909
Dr: Can you tell us more about what they did?
Al: Lizzie. She did it.
Dr: Who is Lizzie?
Al: She took care of me—governess. I was in a crib.
Dr: Where did she spill it?
Al: Down my dress—my chest. Gravy—

Under Henry George's questioning, Al told in the accents of a toddler how he had been burned, how it hurt, how the governess had changed his dress so it wouldn't show. He sounded miserable. The doctor suggested he go back before that.

". . . Sing lullabies," Al mumbled, "Go to sleep my ba-a-by . . ."

Dr. George then urged, "Go back before this, before you were born. You have that power. Go back to your last experience. Tell us where you were. Who you were." Al did not respond until Dr. George urged deeper sleep, complete relaxation adding "Bring these memories up to the surface for us."

"Jack—that was my name, Jack."

"Jack what?"

"Can't remember."

"Tell us more about Jack. You can bring it up."

". . . Carstairs. 1845."

Dr. George decided that was the year of birth.

"Where were you born?"

"Columbus, Ohio. The street was 171 Jackson Avenue."

Before the session, Al and Dr. George had planned together the type of questions that would be asked, to find out not only details that could be checked for Dr. George's research, but what the life seemed to mean, with its stresses and rewards, faults and virtues, love, sin, religion, death.

Speaking as "Jack Carstairs," Al described his father, Samuel Carstairs, a bearded man who wielded a razor strap and worked as a carpenter, and his mother, Ruth. He described the brick school building he attended two blocks from his home, told how he quit school at the age of eight to work on their ten acres, how he went back to school in his early teens to study to be a minister, then quit because he "didn't like it."

He recalled enlisting in the 31st regiment at Decatur, Illinois, as a drummer boy. With a voice of youthful enthusiasm he exclaimed, "I could drum good, too!" He spoke of being in the battles of Manassas and Bull Run, of being wounded in the arm. He recalled the hospital tent and how they poured alcohol over his wound.

Later, Jack came to Philadelphia, where he married a pretty little Chinese girl who was only fifteen. He changed her Chinese name "Ming" to "Sarah" because he felt people were prejudiced against her as an Oriental, and thought the new name would help. Jack and "Sarah" had a love of music in common; she sang a great deal, he played the piano. Chopin was his favorite. They had two children, a son, Robert Earl Carstairs, and a daughter, Alice, who died at birth.

Eventually, he said, they moved to Toronto, where his Chinese wife was accepted socially more easily than in Philadelphia. Jack worked in a mill there but had an accident and lost his right arm. This left him very depressed.

"I didn't want to work anymore."

"And what did you do?"

"I studied."

"What did you study then?"

"Bible."

"Did you believe in reincarnation?"

"No. That's rubbish, I don't believe in that stuff."

He spoke of becoming converted to Catholicism after studying with a religious man, an eminent Catholic, in Boston.

"And did the Catholic priest condone your reading the Bible?"

"I didn't let him know it."

"And what was your goal in life then?"

"Union with God. See, I didn't see it in church, any church."

At one point Henry George asked, "Did you come back into this country—the U.S., that is?"

"Lots of times. Buffalo. I used to have a girl there. Shouldn't do that because I was married."

"And what was her name?"

"Louise. I don't want to talk about that. Shouldn't do that. That's not right."

"What else did you do?"

"That's not right, that's not right!"

After more questions and an urge to deeper relaxation, the sleeper came up with another identity.

"March 29, 1710 . . . I was born . . . (a place sounding like) Chatill Court. Name was Pierre . . ."

"What was your father's name?"

"Pierre."

"What was your mother's name?"

"I can't remember."

Asked if he lived during the French Revolution, "Pierre" protested, "I don't remember—I can't remember anything!" A pause, then he suddenly cried out, "Jesus! Jesus!—appeared in a vision!"

"He appeared to you in a vision?"

"I wish—Couldn't I repeat that vision?" "Pierre" asked plaintively, then murmured, "1715. Five years old—I don't want to remember that."

He balked at recalling any more of that life. Dr. George urged him to go further back. Soon Al muttered that he was a monk in Naples, the year somewhere around 1450 A.D., living part of the time in a cave. Dr. George mentioned the names of a number of noted people of that period, but the monk recalled seeing only one, Michelangelo. He said he had watched him work from a distance. Al was silent when asked some information about his order, then said "It isn't allowed to give."

"How do you pray?"

"Laude, Laude, Patrem . . ." his voice trailed off.

Dr. George then asked if he would like to go back further in time. The sleeping man protested foggily, "I can't seem to find where I am." Gently, encouragingly, the doctor tried to lead him out of the disorientation then urged him further back.

"There is a storm coming up!"

"What kind of storm?"

"Awful storm—" Al's voice sounded something like a frightened child's. "The sky is very black. I am watching—"

"Where are you watching from?"

In a plaintive voice, "You can see it as easy as I can. A storm, awful storm—earthquakes!"

"Does the ground shake?"

"Shaking all over. An awful storm!"

"Is there a volcanic action?"

"No. It's just awful, awful!"

"Where are you?"

"Place called Golgotha. The sky is awful!"

"What are you doing at Golgotha?"

"Standing, watching—" The words almost tumbled out. "A whole lot of people—funny kinds of robes—dirty, filthy, they—dust and—they got all kinds of—Oh, it's awful! You can see them!"

He described a panicky crowd, wind, dust and dirt swirling around. He tried several times to spit as if to clear dirt from his mouth.

"What are they scared of?"

"Thunder, awful noise."

"But there have been thunder storms at Golgotha before. Why should they be afraid of this storm?"

"Something has happened. Something about a man—"

The doctor asked, "Is it a high hill, Golgotha?"

"Yes . . . there's something on top. Three crosses there. All the people are away from it—What are they afraid of? Some woman kneeling at the foot of a cross. Middle, the cross is in the middle. He said, 'Father, forgive them, they know not what they do.' And there isn't anything else there, just a man bleeding. The side of his face is cut. Nails. Look of compassion. Quite a distance, but it seems like I'm right up . . ."

Asked his name, he answered, "Agmesh," later spelling it as A C H M E S H, but he was impatient with the questions, apparently not wanting to leave the scene.

In a puzzled voice, "I don't see the people anymore. Where did all those people go?"

Shaken by what they had witnessed, the group was glad that Dr. George then ended the session and gradually brought Al back to the present. They were all excited. Here was someone who had truly vivid recollections, some of which might be checked out.

Awake, Al felt tired, felt he had been through a straining experience, but when he heard the recording played back, he readily agreed to return for more sessions.

"I want to find out why I'm here," he said, "and what I'm suppossed to be learning in *this* lifetime." He could see some indications from this session. Religion figured prominently in each life period but in different ways. As the most recent, "Jack Carstairs," he had studied the Bible, had even briefly studied for the ministry, but didn't like the work it entailed nor did he later believe in the "rubbish" of reincarnation. Still, he did study with a priest, seeking "union with God" which he had not found in any church. As the French lad "Pierre," he had seen a beautiful vision of Jesus—and died when he was only five. As Achmesh, he witnessed—and felt himself to be part of— the crucifixion scene. Whether or not these lifetimes could be documented or "scientifically" proven was not, for Al, the target question, though it was intriguing. He wanted clues to purpose and meaning, and perhaps would find them from what was being revealed here: the thoughts and feelings of "people" who were within him, whose lives were therefore a part of *his* life.

There were seven succeeding sessions with Dr. George, all of them recorded on wire, then transcribed later by one of two different typists. (One of them had trouble spelling even English words, let alone the foreign words which cropped up frequently. By comparing the sound of the actual voice on the wire recordings with the typewritten text, it has been possible in some cases to correct the typist's errors.)

From time to time Al would spell out his name (for a particular lifetime) or another name for his questioners. (Sometimes a Mr. Herbert Nelson, who was something of a Hebrew scholar, would interrogate, as well as Dr. George.) Sometimes the hypnotized man would tell the questioner he did not remember, but might later come up with the answer.

Sometimes the questioners themselves appeared insufficiently informed—that is, they did not recognize the answer when he gave it. One example was a life when Al recalled being a Roman soldier. Dr. George asked, "What was this month in the Roman Calendar?" Al (who did not know Latin) said, according to one typist, "Ooly" and in a different session with another typist, "Euly." In third-century Latin pronuciation, the month of July would be called "Yu-li," spelled "Juli(us)" [named for Julius Caesar]—apparently what Al was saying. Yet the questioners persisted. "But what is the Roman name for the month?"

What emerged from the series of sessions were nine lives, of which eight were special targets of Dr. George's questioning, to see if any items mentioned could be checked. In reverse chronological order, they included:

—the life of "Jack Carstairs," from about 1845 to 1896, with some experiences in the Civil War, in Philadelphia, in New York and in Toronto.

—The very brief, five-year life of the French lad, "Pierre," around 1715.

—Then the period around 1585 as "James II," son of James I of England, who ran off to France at age 15, had a love affair and a son before his father located him and brought him back to England. Later he helped supervise the translators his father had working on the Bible.

—Around 1450 was the experience as a Jesuit monk near Naples, in Italy.

—From about 929 to 956, one of the happiest lives, as a black man in Tripoli, under the tribal leader Longo, days of singing, dancing, fishing. These days ended when he was killed by a shark.

—There was a bleak existance in an underground village in Siberia from about 778 to 823, as "Gregor". "Gregor" met his end when he fell into a glacial rift and froze to death.

—As a Roman, from about 201 to 280 AD, "Stronges" took part in much bloody slaughter in Gaul. In what is now Venice, the soldier met Brunhilde, a Norse blonde (who was now, the hypnotized man told them, Gladys Davis). She was a strong Christian, he the illegitimate son of a Christian leader, who killed, as he was told to, any who did not believe what they were ordered to believe.

—"Achmesh," of the tribe of Benjamin, was his life from about 2 B.C. to 61 A.D. "Achmesh" had described, with much feeling but no sophistication, scenes from his childhood, from around the temple, even a swim in the Sea of Galilee, as well as the electrifying experience of watching the crucifixion on Golgotha. Later, he listened to Stephen and saw him stoned. "Achmesh" became a follower of Jesus, and his life was ended by crucifixion.

—The earliest life brought out in the sessions was as "Onon", a member of Solomon's council in the tenth century B.C. He recalled helping arrange to import a thousand trees for Mt. Carmel. Also, he said Solomon had told him "that there was a man going to be born who would come into his temple and who would save the world. I told Solomon he didn't know what he was saying."

One of the most informative of sessions was held the evening of July 15, 1952. It also held surprises. As soon as Al was put in a trance he began to speak:

"There is a fire at 13th and Spruce Streets on the third floor. A woman in a blue dress, white dots. Her hair caught on fire. She's throwing a towel around it. There's a ladder going up. She's going to be all right."

"What is the name of the building?" asked the doctor.

"1306 Spruce Street, Philadelphia. It's a house."

(At the end of the session, Dr. George asked again about the woman; Al gave her name as Elise Smith, said she had been treated for burns at Pennsylvania Hospital, Eighth and Spruce Streets, and released. Dr. George then telephoned the hospital, but no one there said she had been admitted.)

During this same session Al said suddenly, "There is an earthquake and a lot of shifting. An area over a hundred miles wide—no water for lots of them." Where was he in space and time? "I'm on the planet Mars. Year 1052."

Mr. Nelson also put questions about the birth and death dates and places of some people whose records he had been unable to find. Al in trance gave dates, cemetery names, in one case even describing the drawer of a cabinet in the cemetery office basement which contained the missing record.

After Dr. George had gone through questions about three of the lifetimes, he asked a question which Al had earlier requested:

"Now I'm going to ask you if it is possible for you to look back on these three experiences as Achmesh, as the Roman and as this man from the North (Gregor). Can you give us the master motive of your lives? Can you see a connection, a reason, a purpose for your having come into each of these forms, and times and peoples? What was the lesson you had to learn? Why were you given the opportunity of living again and again?"

After a long pause, Al replied:

"Each experience was given that this soul might cease to draw farther from God and draw closer . . . The experiences taught this soul that it must have many more experiences to learn to depend less on self utterly.

"In these experiences, the soul entered three bodies. In each of these three bodies, the body tried to dictate to the soul. The soul was . . . dependent on the body. . . . The experiences given were to teach the soul to rely not on the house of the body but completely to rely on the Universal . . . through those experiences that might be necessary . . . in that the body may not be dominant. . . . Those experiences having been lessons in teaching, that the body is not dominant, that the soul is making its way back, and that the body should help—and not dictate. That is the lesson taught this soul."

Al later listened to his own voice on the wire recorder giving the explanations. Was *this* what his four heart attacks had been telling him? He recognized that yearning the hypnotized voice spoke of, the yearning for union with God. It was beginning to make sense, in a confusing sort of way. To strive *not* to be dependent on the body, with its heart attacks and whatever else was to come in this lifetime.

There was so much he could learn from those other lives. Whether or not anyone else could prove he had really lived them, Al felt the reality of the experiences within himself. He remembered growing, trying, working, weeping, loving, dying.

And some of these experiences left vivid marks that became part of him now. One of the most intensely vivid had come in the hypnotic session at Virginia Beach two weeks before, with witnesses who included Hugh Lynn Cayce, David Kahn Jr., Lydia J. Schrader Gray, and Gladys. During this session Al had relived several lives and recalled the end of his life as Achmesh, the Hebrew:

"And how did you meet your end?"

"Crucifixion."

"You were crucified? And what was your offense?"

"*Light.* I saw that this man was the Christ, and I believe it, and they crucified many for that offense, for believing in him." Christ—was the light! He recalled the death of Stephen. "Stephen they stoned. He was the most beautiful person, blue lovely eyes, brown flashing eyelids, matted light brown hair. He wore a belt, red and gold, and he followed and preached the Master . . . and I saw him stoned. What a wonderful way to die, I thought. Stephen and Jesus forgave. I thought his name was the Christ everyone looked for, and they crucified him for it. What more could anyone want than that? Many of us, many of us they crucified, everyone right and left. Paul they crucified upside down, finally. But I was just one of many, happy of the opportunity." To the hypnotized man, it was obviously a pleasure that blotted out the physical.

Even later, when Al closed his eyes, he could sometimes recall a trace of that strange ecstasy more wonderful than life.

To Hugh Lynn Cayce, to Gladys and to the others of the A.R.E., there was nothing particularly surprising about someone having lived during that period or at any other period in the past. Several of those connected with the A.R.E. had been told by the sleeping Edgar Cayce that they had lived during the time, they had been told their names then and some of the experiences they had which affected their present lives. What was important was NOT the living of previous lives, but how the series of lives might indicate the progress (if any) of the soul. What was important was how to live *this* life, using the information from the past where it would be helpful.

Somehow, Al knew, he was supposed to learn not to depend on his body but on God.

Meanwhile, there was a whole new life ready for living. Gladys had said "Yes."

They would be married in July.

X
Smilin' Al

New happiness surrounded Al like an aura visible to his Virginia Beach friends. Mary Ellen Carter[1] wrote of Al as "the kind of man who made it easy for one to forget the imperfections of life and to concentrate on the moment at hand as if it were sacred. Which he thought it was. He had a smile that opened up his face and came through his brown eyes like sunshine through browned stained glass. He stored jokes like a squirrel stores little acorns and when he told them, he enjoyed them more than anybody."

This delighted Gladys. Serious as she was about her work, she had a lively sense of humor for other things, keeping track of the clever remarks of little nieces and nephews and others, seasoning her letters and converstaions with the peppery anecdotes. Laughter sparkled around Glad Niche like sunlight on the waves.

There was a lull in the schedule at A.R.E. headquarters; many people had left on vacations; the congress crowd had gone.

They planned to be married on July 19th. Gladys's friend, Lydia J. Schrader Gray, asked them to have the ceremony in her apartment. "But the date has very bad vibrations," she warned. (Lydia was a numerologist.) "Have it before or after, but not *on* the 19th!"

They compromised. The wedding party gathered in Lydia's apartment on Saturday evening, July 19, 1952. The bride wore a paisley print of light blue which highlighted her blue eyes and blond hair. Sheila Kennedy, a friend of Al's from Philadelphia, sang "O Promise Me." With Gladys and Al, participating in the ceremony were her sister Lucille, her husband Shay and Gladys's nephew "T.J." (Thomas Jefferson) Davis. But it was until half past midnight—or half an hour into the new date of July 20—that the Rev. Robert P. Davis of the

---

[1] Mary Ellen Carter wrote a biography of Gladys, published in 1972 as *My Years with Edgar Cayce*, "The Story of Gladys Davis Turner," updated and reissued in 1985 as *Miss Gladys and the Edgar Cayce Legacy*.

First Presbyterian Church pronounced Al and Gladys man and wife.

In the midst of festivities, Al whispered to Gladys, "There's an extra brightness about you. Maybe you'll laugh—but I see angels!" Gladys saw tears in his eyes. Nobody laughed.

It should have been idyllic: the married life begun in the little cottage surrounded by fragrant camellias and gardenias, even with its own vine and fig tree. But two shadows hung over it.

One which was readily identified was the strain of Al's weekly commuting to Philadelphia to the offices of Auchincloss, Parker and Redpath. A seven-hour drive on each end of a weekend was exhausting and the five days between were lonely. But conviction that they were on the right course sustained them through the difficulties of readjustments. For Gladys, there was no change of home or job; she continued as Secretary of the A.R.E., continued her work indexing the readings and workings with Cayce materials. Though she did not travel often, she did make an effort to go with Al on some busines trips, one of which they'd never forget.

On this particular night they were returning to Virginia Beach from Philadelphia. "In our little Chevrolet sedan," Gladys recalled,

> . . . after eating at Delaware diner, we were taking turns driving. Around 11 o'clock I was taking a nap on the back seat. The first thing I knew, I had rolled off the seat onto the floor. Al had seen a big truck coming right at him, lights blazing. He had gone off the road at a level place. He turned and was able to get back on the highway. We looked around and found that if we had gone off the road before or after that spot, we would have gone down a steep bank and we would have been killed. We felt so protected!

Although he survived the commuting, Al arranged gradually to phase out his Philadelphia activities. He found it next to impossible to transplant his investment banking to Virginia Beach, but the Beach was more important. By the end of 1952, he had finished with his "Philadelphia connection" and had a little office behind the garage of Glad Niche.

The other shadow, not so easily identified, was more frightening as a result. Inexplicable, troubling incidents. One time, leaving the bus station platform, Al noticed a woman in a plaid coat, saw a dark figure lunge from the shadow and snatch her pocketbook—then realized she still had it. Impulsively he reached forward and touched her elbow.

"Pardon me, but you'd better watch your pocketbook." He wanted to tell her what he had "seen" but wasn't quite sure how to put it. The woman drew away from him with a sharp grimace.

"You mind your own business. Don't touch me again or I'll call a cop!"

Al stepped back. In a few minutes he heard the woman scream. He knew what had happened. Why did he know it?

There was the time the brown-haired matron came down the post office steps. He knew she was going to get into a car that was about to be struck by a taxi. Urgently he spoke to her,

"Excuse me, Miss. Please don't get in that car!"

She was startled, indignant. "What's wrong with you? You crazy or something?" she snapped as she got in her friend's car. Al felt as if *he'd* been struck when he heard the crash two minutes later.

These experiences kept happening. "Men, women, even children—I can see awful things before they happen to them but I can't prevent it," Al confessed to Gladys. "When I warn people, they think I'm crazy!"

Gladys was concerned, but suggested, "Our friends Bob and Les are coming over. Why don't you all play some pinochle? That should take your mind off of this problem for a while."

When Bob and Les came over, they happily agreed to a game of cards. As the dealing began, Al felt cheerful and almost his old self again. But then, as each player took up his hand, Al looked about him, puzzled, and mopped his brow. "I can't play with you fellows," he said expressionlessly.

"Why not? Did you forget to mark the cards?" Bob kidded.

"Sure we're good," Les joked, "but you shouldn't get discouraged so quick."

"It isn't that," Al muttered, "It's no good. I know what you've got."

"No way," Bob retorted.

Al drew a breath. "You've a queen, ten, nine of spades, a pair of aces . . ." and he went on to name every card each of them held. They stared at him.

Gladys came over and laid a comforting hand on his shoulder. Al was doing no "magic trick," he was seriously worrried at this unwanted awareness. He was, somehow, able to tell what was on those cards even when he could not see them. There was no fun left in the game. The conversation that had begun lightheartedly became mired in puzzled concern.

Finally Bob got up to leave. Al held out a restraining hand. "Be careful. A flat tire—as you're going over the bridge." Bob shrugged. An hour later Bob phoned from his home. Yes, there had indeed been a flat. In the rain. And he had had to change it, and had only now reached home. "Thanks a lot," he added sardonically as if Al had somehow given him the flat.

Alone with Gladys, Al spoke openly about his fears that he might continue to have these unwanted connections with other people's misfortunes, to "know" what would happen and feel the agony of being unable to prevent it. And he might continue to "know" what cards people held, information which took the pleasure out of the card games. Wryly he commented, "Some folks would say I ought to use this to make money at cards—but I couldn't!"

Gladys nodded. She remembered that Edgar Cayce, whenever someone had misused his trance abilities for profits got very ill; this was before his wife had taken over as the "conductor" of the readings, screening the questions to avoid such misuse.

"When I said I wanted to have psychic abilities," Al groaned, "I didn't mean *this*!" This kind of precognition added unsettling misery to daily contacts. "I don't know what turned it on," he cried out in frustration, "I just want to turn it off!"

Gladys reminded him that he had for some years been trying "exercises" from the Rosicrucians and others to develop psychic ability.

"But why should they start working all of a sudden?"

"Do you suppose," Gladys asked, "that your repeatedly being hypnotized and regressed to these different lifetimes might have helped to open up some awareness center in the brain? Perhaps this combination—the hypnosis plus the 'exercises'—might have brought it on?"

Al did not know. But it was a reasonable suggestion.

"What did Edgar Cayce say about developing psychic ability?"

There were many who had asked the sleeping Cayce about developing their own psychic powers. Gladys promised to look up some of the readings on the subject the next day.

One man had asked: "Are there any exercises you can give me for the development of my faculty of intuition?"

The reply: "Much might be given, but ye are ready for little of same yet. Find first thy relationships to thy Maker." Concerning that

65

relationship, he referred often to Deuteronomy 30 and its statement that God's word "is not hidden from thee, neither is it far off . . . I have set before you life and death . . . therefore choose . . ." Edgar Cayce continued to advise, in trance, "Pursue, rather, spiritual development; this is of the psychic nature, yes, but find the spirit first—not spiritualism, but spiritually in thine own life." (3460–1)

Together, Gladys and Al decided he would have no more of the hypnotic regression sessions after the next one which had already been scheduled for August 14 in Wilmington. Al had already given up the earlier psychic development exercises. He echoed another reading: "Development of the soul and ideals must come first."

Still, it was three long years before the shadow lifted and Al was able to meet with people as an ordinary friend, without the occasional flashes of horror at the misery hiding in the future.

***

Meanwhile the sheer joy of being in Virginia Beach with the woman he loved more than made up for the other problems. Al's enthusiasm for the area shows in a later letter to his artist-sister-in-law, Billie, written the day after Christmas; " 'Tis good by oceanside here. Whistling winds around the house. *No place* on earth is more beautiful Starting in January, something is in bloom *always*, 365 days a year, with cold weather Sasanquas and Daphnes out now—beautiful to paint."

Perhaps because of the Eden-like atmosphere there, Al found few customers for investments. In fact, making money seemed, if anything, more difficult here than in Philadelphia. He decided to study for a real estate license to add to other skills.

"Why don't you try something you really like to do?" was Gladys's question. "You have a way with flowers." It was true, he had always liked plants, especially flowers, and had always been happy working with them.

They purchased a greenhouse, set it up on the front lawn, stacked it with plants, and "GLAD GARDENS" was born. Cheerful post cards were sent out

```
              GLAD GARDENS
              Smilin' Al Offers

CARNATIONS         CANDYTUFT              GERANIUMS
PETUNIAS           COWSLIPS               SCARLET SAGE
ALYSSUM            PANSIES                AZALEAS
  White              Giant                  Dwarf

Basket of Gold
              And any available perennials or annuals
                        IN QUANITY
                will sell any of these plants
                 PLANTED for YOU by SMILIN' AL
         Make a date now for planting before the spring rush.

                      Phone for Estimate

1871-M              ALWAYS OPEN              300 14th St.
```

Al's personality began to bloom. Working with the flowers not only didn't tire him, it actually refreshed him. His smile became something of a trademark. His "Happy Birthday" greeting first surprised and then intrigued the growing circle of friends and customers. "We're born again every day," Al happily explained to everyone who asked him about it, "and we have a new opportunity every day, so why not say Happy Birthday?" They'd shake their heads, smiling and agreeing in spite of themselves.

In the house, on the wall beside his bed, was a "Meditation" Al had typed up, one which he reread each morning:

THIS IS THE DAY THAT THE LORD HATH MADE.
LET US BE GLAD AND REJOICE IN IT. (Psalm 118:24)

May this day be bright and beautiful in every way for me. May every hour hold happiness; may every experience of this day be enriching and rewarding. May every person I meet this day receive a blessing from me and leave a blessing with me.

May this day hold for me healing. May I know and feel the wonderful healing power of God, mighty and strong *within* me. May this day I feel filled with life and health and strength. May I radiate a blessing of health and healing to others this day; may all those persons around me be helped and healed through my healing faith.

May this day be a growth for me, a day in which I see myself as a child of God learning and progressing and growing on the path of life. May this day be a day of appreciation by me of all that has gone before, of all the ways in which I have learned to grow; a day of appreciation by me of all the blessings that are right at hand, the good that surrounds me constantly, *always*. Bless me this day, to THY service, in making others happy.

Al began collecting sayings, maxims on beauty and nature, the way legendary King Midas collected gold. Some favorites:

Every seed is a longing.
We live only to discover beauty. All else is a form of waiting.
If you sing of beauty, though alone in the desert, you will have an audience.
You see but your shadow when you turn your back to the sun.

Al added a couple of beehives to the gardens of Glad Niche. One acquaintance asked what a man of his obvious scholarly background was doing tending flowers and raising bees. Al smiled with the quick reply, "It's one of the easiest ways to spread beauty and love!" but the words and their implications set him to musing while he worked. Later he went in to his typewriter and tapped out:

So long as the bee is outside the petals of the flower, it buzzes and emits sounds. But when it is inside the flower, the sweetness thereof has silenced and overpowered the bee. Forgetful of sounds and itself, it drinks the nectar in quiet.

Men of learning, you too are making a noise in the world. But know, the moment you get the slightest enjoyment of the sweetness of bhakti,[2]

---

[2]Bhakti—Webster's: [Hinduism:] Religious devotion; love directed towards a personal deity.—The Hindu World: Bhakti: Attachment or fervent devotion to God; Fr. Bhaga—[Orthodox] Personal god of love, mercy and peace to devotees; total self-surrender to will of divinity of human soul.)

you will be like the bee in the flower, inebriated with the nectar of divine love.

Are too many people in the world making noises when flowers of silence are countless blessings around us?

"That's beautiful!" Gladys exclaimed. she encouraged his writing.

Since the natural world was so close to God, Al often used plants and flowers to express regard, gratitude and affection. He would present friend after friend with a plant, often telling a bit of a story about the plant at the same time.

Al's appreciation of the beauty of silence also showed in his helping the Virginia Beach Friends' Meeting to get started. Although Gladys attended the First Presbyterian Church, and Al had gone with her at times, in 1954 he joined the Friends' Meeting. A bit later he commented in a letter to Billie, "it's funny; all the Quaker Meetings at Pocono, at Haverford, at Merion, etc., I never appreciated nor even attended. Now at this late date the significance of Inwardness is apparent." Here, to the Friends' Meeting House on Laskin Road, he would bring a gardenia bush whenever he could, until the modest building was almost framed by them. The fragrant flowers' beauty, he felt, spoke silently to "that of God within." In the next couple of years, Al bought an acre of land for the Virginia Beach Friends' School, paying for it a bit at a time. He was so glad that Gladys, instead of nagging him for "wasting" money that could have gone for the household expenses, supported him in these generous feelings.

Going into real estate was another venture Al enjoyed: showing lots and parts of this Beach he had come to love, to friendly folk who might make their homes here. Though he was a bit in awe of Hugh Lynn Cayce, the chairman of A.R.E. and Edgar Cayce's oldest son, he was still glad to be able to work with him in some of the real estate activities.

One of Al's great delights was talking with the young children in the neighborhood, as well as Gladys's little nephew Michael, who called her "Granny." The tots swarmed around Glad Niche as bees around the gardenias.

"Mr. Flower Man!" was a frequent cry when a child would spy Al by his greenhouse, "Mr. Flower Man!" Al would respond with a quick smile. His natural love for children had never found much expression before. He enjoyed them, liked to give them flowers, but more than that, Gladys recalled, "He taught them about nature, to understand it and respect it. He had been saddened when some children tore the leaves off our mimosa tree and it died. Instead of yelling and scolding, Al explained to the children about how plants grow, how to take care of them so they bear fruit. From time to time he would give them some, such as the figs or grapes. They really learned from him."

One child in particular, little Walter Rountree, would toddle over from his home along the side of the lake to see "Mr. Flower Man" and just talk about anything and everything. At first his mother, wondering where he was, would come out and call him—but soon she knew just where to find him. She, too, would stop and visit "Mr. Flower Man." Al felt unusually drawn to little Walter; his lively affection and the look in his eyes were both warm and familiar. Was it possible he had known him before?

Testing his theory, Al used "Paul" in his conversation a few times. Each time, Walter responded as if that were his name. Al confided to Gladys that it was a beautiful feeling that his brother Paul could have come back to share affection and companionship.

Children, in fact, received the same warm respect from both Gladys and Al as did their adult friends, and they usually responded in kind. One day John Doughty stopped by, and Al and Gladys urged him and the two with him, one a lad about thirteen, to come in and "Sit down, make yourselves at home!" The conversation was lively but the lad seemed ill at ease. Finally Gladys asked him, "Is something the matter?" The lad blurted out, "I just came to collect for the paper!"

Another day, the phone rang. Gladys recognized the voice of little Stephen: "Gladys, I've got bad news for you!" Anxiously, Gladys waited. Had something happened to his grandmother, her good friend? To him?

"I frowed up!" he finished. She sighed with sympathy and relief. Being warmly accepted by children carried its own problems.

Al's cheerfulness was reaching an ever-growing circle. Star of the Sea Catholic Church was across the street from Glad Niche, and a home for the nuns was almost adjacent to the vines and fig trees Al had cultivated while he quoted Micah (4.4), "But they shall sit every man under his vine and under his fig tree; and none shall make them afraid . . ." As the nuns passed back and forth along the path near his garden, Al would blithely greet each one, "Happy Birthday, Sister!" At first they did not know what to make of it, but eventually began to smile and return the greeting.

Even the priest of Star of the Sea, Father Nicholas J. Habets, regularly exchanged greetings with Al and Gladys. Al's greetings and cards were more humorous sometimes than one might consider proper for a prelate. After one such card, received on his seventy-first birthday, Father Habets wrote to thank Al and Gladys

> . . . for the funniest birthday card ever seen. Not that I mind my age—71—I'm rather proud of it—but you are so loyal not to give away a secret. I may say that I have enjoyed 12 happy years with you as neighbors. God bless you.
>
> Sincerely,
> Fr. N. Habets

HAPPY BIRTHDAY

It was beautiful to be able to spread the message, "Happy Birthday! We're born again!"—to spread seeds of friendship and have them blossoming all around, to be active and happy.

***

XI
Blessed Are Those . . .

There were places it was difficult to spread a message, particularly a happy message. In May of 1956 Al had a letter from his niece Doris that her father, Brinkley, was very ill with cancer. He immediately went north to Brinkley's home in Wynnewood, near Philadelphia. There he sat and spoke awhile with Billie and Doris. Then he went upstairs to find his brother sitting in the room that had been his favorite, "the library," its walls lined with books. That gaunt figure sitting in the old college lounge chair had been his powerful brother; the figure sat, restless, talking—but not to the one in front of him. He seemed not to be aware of what was going on, just talking bitterly about—it was impossible to say what. Al prayed that he might sense the right thing to say and do; he prayed tht his brother would find whatever was best for him.

When he came back down the stairs, Al returned to Billie and Doris, held their hands in his and assured them, "He is going to be all right." The two women looked at each other. How could Al possibly say such a thing?

Before he left them, Al gave Doris his copy of *There is a River* to read.

June 6, Brinkley died.

Later, Doris confided to Al, "When you told me that Papa was going to be 'all right,' I thought you really didn't know what you were saying. But when he died, about five minutes after we closed his eyes, Mother and I were standing together in the bedroom and I felt a hand on my shoulder. Mother looked at me. She felt something, too. I heard the words, 'My girls'—and asked her if she had heard them. She had! It was Papa's fondest way of referring to us. We both *knew*, then, that he was out of that cancerous body. He was truly *all right!*"

Doris then began reading the story of Edgar Cayce, finding it at first unbelievable until, through Al, she met some of the people in it, particulary Gladys.

In Virginia Beach, meanwhile, there was much excitement at A.R.E.

as Headquarters was moved from the Cayce home to the roomier former hospital building on the hill at 67th Street.

Al now was making friends in many places; he was using his flowers and plants, making the Friends' Meeting, the A.R.E. areas, and other gardens more beautiful; he was making progress helping organize groups and classes—he was making everything, in fact, except money. He had tried. In 1955, he and Gladys had even formed the "Organicus Company," with Al as president, Gladys as secretary, to offer gardening supplies and assistance. Though the plants grew, the company didn't. Even Glad Gardens brought in more happiness than income. Reluctantly, Al let his work with plants become a sideline. He kept on with his real estate work, but in addition began working for the Norfolk Post Office as a sub-clerk.

Rather than feel depressed, he saw this as a new opportunity for making friends and trying to spread some of the happiness he was enjoying. The other workers at first found this fellow whose daily greeting was "Happy Birthday" odd, but soon felt his friendliness. Appreciation was mutual.

For his part, Al was quite proud of the way they managed the mail in spite of obstructions and hindrances the general public knew nothing about. He would tell Gladys, at home in the evening, about some of the incidents—the stove parts and dead snakes found in the mail boxes—and she would encourage him to write about them. So Al read up on postal facts and history and typed out "What's Right With the Post Office,"an article which opened with ancient ways of sending mail, then included a tour of the Norfolk Post Office on a typical day:

> Let us go first to the setup table where your letter, with hundreds of thousands of others, is dumped onto the table from mail bags and carts as it is taken from post box. Often it is said that 'everything but the kitchen stove' comes out of the post box. Once, here in Norfolk, even parts of the kitchen stove were dumped onto the facing table! Yes, people put all kinds of things into the mailbox besides mail: empty and half-full gin bottles, old shoes, dead snakes, dead cats, evangelistic tracts by the hundreds—and these are taken right out to the setup table and dumped in the clerks' laps, literally.
>
> Now, let's examine the letters.
>
> We find many of these letters, perhaps hundreds in an evening, with no address at all! Do you now blame the post office so much for not delivering that letter you mailed and Joe Dokes never got? Yes, hundreds

of people daily put letters in the box with no address at all. Well, we can always send them back to the senders—or can we? Most of these unaddressed letters also have no return address!

Readers of the article would have to admire the ingenuity and dedication of the postal workers for their accomplishments under the circumstances! Al wrote another article, entitled "Speed Your Mail," starting with a history of the post from Biblical times and references, e.g. "Now my days are swifter than a post," (Job 9:25)

Al's fellow employees enjoyed them. Editors returned them.

The Norfolk Post Office workers now nicknamed him "Happy Birthday" in friendly kidding. Al grew to know the men as individuals, their problems and hopes, and worked and joked and talked with them just as openly about God's love as about the weather . . . until his coworkers no longer felt hesitant but actually at home with the topic.

Life seemed serene: he had Gladys, friends, work, health. Then in 1958 another heart attack struck, with a minor stroke. This time he had the prayers and support of hosts of friends, even the boys and girls in the Friends' School, to whom he had often talked about plants, the beauty of growing things.

His friend Louise Wilson remembers, "When he returned home from the hospital, Al came to the Friends' School to thank everyone for their prayers. He sat in a chair and gave a packet of seeds to every student."

Unlike his convalescence from those attacks in Philadelphia, here Al's meditation, his intoning a *mantra,* or talking of the *kundalini* rising along the *chakras* upset no one. Here his friends did not consider him strange for his desire to use words from other languages or religions when they seemed more specific than their English equivalent. They accepted as normal his closing letter to them with *Agape,* the Greek word for the love of one human being for another (as differing from the love of a man for a woman, child for parent, etc.). This acceptance speeded his recovery.

Shortly after returning home, Al said he wanted to go back to work at the post office. Gladys cautioned, "You need to be careful not to do too much." Al protested; there was no way he could do too much if it involved helping with their joint finances. Gladys's modest salary had been taking care of the two of them whenever his income stopped; he wanted to contribute more as long as he was physically able.

Still, there was that warning from the past-lives regression, that the soul should not rely on the body but on the Universal, on God. Al pondered, then determined to go back to work, but also to increase his reliance on the Spirit.

Every day was beginning with increasing energy, from the first physical moments in the bathroom, where opposite the "seat of reflection" Al had taped on the wall: daily meditations from the readings, special thoughts, and the names of persons he and Gladys were praying for. "Love *is* creative," he said, "When you give more, you have more to give!"

The strength came back, the needed strength to continue his work for the Norfolk Post Office, as well as occasional real estate work, plus his greenhouse and flowers on the side. Evenings and weekends he shared some time with Gladys in ARE activities, lectures, study group meetings, meditations, prayer group meetings. He continued his study of the Book of Revelation wherever he could fit in the time. His mind kept leaning to so many topics that tugged at his interests: reincarnation in the Bible, the effect of color in therapy, in life and in religion, and the need for inner peace. He made notes, filed away references, but there simply was not enough time to complete any of these studies.

He wanted and needed to get deeper into what the Study Groups of the ARE called "A Search for God." Most of the time he felt he was on the right path, but sometimes it was as if the path was on the edge of a cliff; he felt his very human failings could send him crashing. Emotional intensity sharpened his feelings. One warm day, a line from one of the readings held his attention: "You can only be saved from *self*, there is no other salvation." Al went into deep meditation, then with a pen on notebook paper, wrote:

July 30, 1960

Dear God,

This world we live in is troubled. I would like to eliminate my ego completely and become love itself that starting with myself I can be of the greatest service to Thee. May Jesus Christ dominate and fill me.

       Love,
       Albert E. Turner

Everything was still for a moment. Then as if in a trance, he felt his hand begin to move, and write on the lower half of the paper,

Dear Albert,

> Your every request is granted
> if
> you first seek me
> hourly
> at least

He felt as if he was waking, then read the words as if someone else had written them, then found his eyes filled with tears. Finally, though his voice was a bit choked, he was able to tell Gladys, to show her. Gladys put her arm around him, and agreed softly, "That is beautiful." Now, Al felt certain that being with Gladys gave him his closest communication with God and with that spirit described in the readngs as "the Christ Consciousness."

It was from this moment on that, in writing or typing his correspondence, Al always referred to himself with a small "i" rather than the capital "I." Some people commented that they found this a bit confusing, but Al believed this was part of his program towards selflessness.

Searching for more ways to strengthen his spiritual path, Al decided to try "living" the Sermon on the Mount, taking one thought to focus on each day. He began this discipline on January 10, 1961 and kept a journal of the results.

Some excerpts:

1. January 10. Matt. 5:3. Blessed are the poor in spirit for theirs is the kingdom of heaven. . . . Noted people who were "braggadocios", that is, very loud, were attracted to me and i in soft-spokenness changed their braggadociousness; i, in turn, am very loud daily. In trying to be cheerful i make a lot of noise; today i was very quiet, and observant, trying to catch little things i could do for people.

2. January 11, Matt. 5:4. Blessed are they that mourn, for they shall be comforted. . . . Each verse in the Sermon on the Mount has its individual interpretation for everyone; this is only my experience; i tried to bring into consciousness many times . . . daily verse, and to pass it along to . . . others. Here is what happened to me each day as each verse was repeated: Today, countless people seemed to ready my mind, anticipating my needs! . . . In driving to Norfolk and back every traffic light was green, perhaps fifty during the day! Also there seemed to be joyousness around me in *every single person i met!*

3. January 12, Matt. 5:5. Blessed are the meek, for they shall in-

herit the earth. 1. Everything "right" happened for and to me today. 2. Many times the right thing popped out from my voice without thinking. 3. Found that this verse was marvelous in supplanting negative thoughts.

    8. January 17. Matt. 5:9. Blessed are the peacemakers, for they shall be called the children of God. Had peace within. David Bromley's father "out of danger." He was overjoyed. His dad had been on the top of our prayer list. Reading on sharing points out this necessity of peace within for healing. One of the people to whom it was given said, "This is what salvation is"—the peace within.

    13. January 22. Matt. 5:15: Let your light so shine before men that they may see thy good works and glorify thy Father which is in Heaven. Went today to hear Zip Johnson, coworker at the P.O., speak at negro Baptist Church for the first time in his life—a speech which was as beautiful as any i ever heard. Truly Zip today was this verse!

    15. January 25. Matt. 5:20. For except your righteousness exceed the righteousness of the scribes and the Pharisees, ye shall in no way enter into the kingdom of Heaven. i repeated this to two others and found i was trying to "give it away" instead of apply it!

    26. February 4. Matt. 5:44. Love your enemies, bless them that curse you, do good to them that hate you and pray for them which despitefully use you and persecute you. . . . Was given a test on this, was bawled out underservingly. i blessed the supervisor, went to him, agreeably talked over things and i am sure his attitude became friendly.

Al castigated himself on February 12, writing,

> "i must be going through a cleansing; things have been mentally rough for three days; can't say I was good as a result of verses or applications, as i don't believe i applied."

For February 13, he had chosen Matt. 6:19, "Lay not up for yourselves treasures upon earth, where moth and rust doth corrupt, and where thieves break through and steal." "Treasures upon earth"— Was that what he was working so hard for, at the post office? Of course not. He almost laughed at the thought. He just wanted to give HIS share of income to their home. But he never got to "apply" that verse.

Instead, there was the straining pain, the collapse. The ambulance rushed him to the hospital, where he found himself in the cloudy world of numbness, confusion, helplessness.

Why? The grim question hung in the air. Why would God do this to him when he had been trying so hard to seek Him? Then it was as if he heard an echo from the recording of his voice in trance:

> "The experiences given were to teach the soul to rely not on the hosue of the body but completely to rely on the Universal . . . that the soul is making its way back, and that the body should help—and not dictate. . . ."

There was no way, now, that the body could dictate.

XII
Learning, Love, Laughter

Slowly, one muscle, one joint, one finger at a time, Al was regaining the power to move. He *willed* his fingers, his feet, to do what the therapist said. Sometimes his mental command had no result, sometimes there was a bend of a finger, of a wrist, an occasion for celebration! When Gladys came for her daily visit, he would demonstrate a new movement, a new gesture, then see the sparkle in her eyes and glow on hearing her delighted praise. It spurred him. His speech was coming back too. Even the doctor began to admit that Al might not always be wheelchair bound.

Towards the end of April he was able to return home. Gladys set a contour reclining chair where Al could sit and take part in friendly gatherings—or take a nap.

With his body forced into quiet by the stroke, Al found his thoughts more active than ever. It took mental wrestling to pull them into line. There had to be some good come out of this. What a challenge to look for it!

Letters and warm wishes did more than vitamins to speed his returning strength. Another letter from his post office friend "Zip" Johnson came:

> "... I must say you are the most remarkable man I have met during my lifetime (55 years). And I admit that you have been a source of great encouragement to me for a long time now. You have been a source of great inspiration and continue to be an outstanding example of "The Greatest Thing in the World"—Love ..."

Al sighed and shook his head. Gladys remonstrated, "Why on earth should you look so sad when he sends you a letter like that?"

"He shouldn't say that about me," Al muttered, "I've made so many mistakes." But gradually, as the message sank in, his lips spread into a glowing grin. "Isn't 'Zip' wonderful to want to help others this way!"

He continued to ponder. There had to be more to come out of this than just being a recipient for others' kindnesses, the receiver that made the givers "more blessed." One afternoon, waiting for Gladys to help him out of his chair, he suddenly laughed aloud. Gladys hurried over, concerned. Al explained wryly, "I've found it! One good thing this stroke has done!" As she helped him along, he added, "Now I really have to depend on the spirit, and not the body."

One of the first things he did when he was again able to form words with his pen was to take up the journal of the Sermon on the Mount, writing:

> LAY NOT UP FOR YOURSELVES TREASURES . . . i was given at the point of death great understanding of this. Had a chance to practice this as 'receiver' for many weeks for hundreds of people were kind and threw love upon me in every way imaginable, laying up for themselves treasures in heaven.

There were so many! Joe Fiutko, who brought carrot juice every night, Juliet, who came almost daily to help, Lydia, whose cards arrived with every mail . . . Friend after friend after friend. He wrote,

> . . . it was like i was surveying this planet from afar and no money was worth anything, no treasures. The only treasure is in heaven, such as "What had i done to help others?" It was as if i felt this, it was not said to me, and no answer was coming from me, none at all! It was as if i was given another chance to live for others, even as hundreds lived for me in kindness.
>
> May 3. Matt. 6:25. Therefore I say unto you, take no thought for your life . . . Thoughts of worry entered my mind, the opposite of the above! After God has brought me through a heart attack (and stroke) i am now more aware of the ridiculousness of worry about the future. Also i need to pray each day for this day only. "This is the day the Lord hath made."
>
> May 11. Matt. 6:28. And why take ye thought concerning raiment. Consider the lilies of the field . . . Lydia visited, and said Mr. Cayce once told her, "Even lilies, Lydia, have their feet in the mud."
>
> May 24. Matt. 6:31. Therefore take no thought . . . i asked Edward to roll the grass seed on the lake side. At 4 A.M. i woke up, realized the water had been on all night. He must have filled the roller and left the water running! It kept me awake the rest of the night even though i said to myself many Bible chapters proved to me the uselessness of worrying about something after it had happened . . . It seems so futile

in view of [the fact that] my life had just been saved, preserved by God!

June 2. Matt. 7:6. Cast not your pearls before swine. Nothing wrong with pearls; nothing wrong with swine. Neither understands the other . . . i found myself talking with everyone on the basis of their understanding. i think this is what is meant to me by Jesus' parables: He was talking in the way people understood.

July 7. Matt. 7:17 through 7:20. Even so every good tree bringeth forth good fruit . . . Found myself without prior thinking giving a message in Friends' Meeting about "the only thing we have is what we have given away" and "these are the fruits of the spirit, the only thing we possess, and the only thing we can give."

As Al shuffled and stumbled, trying to use a cane with his weakened leg, every movement was a struggle. But when it was successful—what a feeling! Al recalled these feelings three years later when their friend, Dr. Frank Moeser, suffered a severe stroke. Al wrote him:

Dear Frank:

Please forgive the paper [notebook paper] but it illustrates a point. I was recently informed you had had a stroke. From my experience, the paper illustrates my point of appreciation of the little things of life, such as a piece of paper, even one with holes in it!

I immediately placed your name on my hourly prayer list; I hope you don't mind!

My own experience—in 1937, Dr. Kohlas of Bryn Mawr, Penna., gave me a year to live, after a heart attack; from then until 1950, three more occurred, each one worse. In spite of this, my condition improved! Then in the 1960s I had two strokes, each one giving me a greater appreciation of LIFE, of the little things in life: a rose, a petal, even a blade of grass, a bird song, a duckling, a spider, yes, a piece of paper with holes in it—EVERYTHING, particularly people.

But the Biblical injunction that God hath not given us anything we are not able to bear has proved as true in my case as anyone's.

Instead of the "joy" of accumulation of "things," a much greater joy comes, it seems to me, with a stroke: that is, the joy of accumulation of moving parts of the body! Each day . . . there comes with effort a new experience—of moving a finger, a joint, a muscle unused for long, a joy transcendental!

One side of mine was completely paralyzed; months later, this went away. 'Twas a lot of fun. What greater fun can there be than the new, found-again ability to move parts of the body?—and most of all, to be re-reminded that people care!

Blessings and Light and Love suround you always,

                Agape,
                Albert

Yes, *this* was another "good," another asset. He could now understand what many other stroke victims went through. He treasured these assets, because there were times, whether alone in his chair or lying awake in the weak hours of the night, when worrisome words wound through his mind: "No more job—no more work—no more paychecks . . . you're just a burden . . . What good are you now?"

And the only way to stop them was to try to find another asset, another good, and to thank God when he did.

Gladys understood more than Al put into words. Without being obtrusive, she encouraged him to keep reaching a little farther, doing just a little bit more, each day. As he increased his effort, Al gained increasing skills. Came the day when he was able to lift himself, from the chair, then go to the next room all by himself, with just the cane!

Now Gladys encouraged Al to come with her each morning when she drove to A.R.E. Headquarters to work. She reminded him that he had already done valuable research and writing for A.R.E. In the enforced idleness after his 1958 hospitalization he had collected material and written an article for the *Searchlight*, a monthly A.R.E. publication, on the topic, "Is Reincarnation in the Bible?" (It was published in two parts, the first in December 1958, the second in April 1960.)

It was some satisfaction for Al that he could use the time which he would have spent working at the post office, if healthy, helping the A.R.E. instead. He enjoyed researching the readings, culling thousands of quotations on the Bible, on music as therapy, on peace (a special concern ever since he had joined the Society of Friends) and on his favorite topic, *The Revelation*.

Al ensconced himself in the basement of the old Headquarters building in an area they often called "the chicken coop" because of its chicken-wire wall barrier, which set it apart from the regular flow of people yet at the same time left it open to communication. In it he had a desk and chair. He had his little portable typewriter with which he would peck out pages of material. Beside the desk was a canvas cot where he would nap when he needed to recoup his strength.

ALBERT AT HIS DESK IN "THE CHICKEN COOP", where he researched the readings, Bible passages and other writings.

Another facet of this arrangement was that Al was in frequent contact with more and more people. Not just those (and there were many) who made a special effort to see him, but also those who visited the various offices quartered in the basement in increasing numbers as the A.R.E. membership and activities expanded. A passer-by on the other side of the chicken wire had no trouble catching a welcoming smile from Al as he looked up from his work.

On the screen door entrance of his "coop" Al tacked a 3 X 5 card with the admonition:

PLEASE CLOSE
BOTH DOORS

At first puzzled by the seeming impossibility of closing "both" doors when there was only one, a visitor would eventually realize there was also a mental door to the outer confusion that needed closing. When sitting down talking with Al, a visitor would somehow find himself in a different, warmer, wider world, a world held up not by Atlas but by the readings, the Bible and love. He would leave the "chicken coop" a bit happier for the experience.

Sometimes Al seemed to be especially sensitive, to know without being told how someone was feeling or whether help was needed. One day Charlotte McMillion, a librarian and friend of Al and Gladys, was walking past when Al looked up. He gave her his "Happy Birthday!" and invited her to pause and talk for a moment. There was no way that he could have learned how badly she needed that moment. He did not know that her husband of thirty-seven years had abruptly broken the news that he was leaving her. Charlotte appeared to enjoy the talk but said little beyond the fact that she was leaving Virginia Beach to return to Philadelphia.

That night Al wrote to a Philadelphia friend, Wilmer Alice Adams, with whom he had shared many thoughts in the past. He asked her, "Please get in touch with Charlotte McMillion. She needs you."

Wilmer Alice Adams phoned Charlotte and invited her to dinner; the two women hit it off right away. Not long afterwards Wilmer introduced Charlotte to a friend, Birley Schoen, who emphasized that he was a confirmed bachelor.

That was great, Charlotte said emphatically, because she herself was just finding out how good it was to be independent. Forget the wedding bells—being "just friends" was fine.

Two years later they were married.

When Charlotte and Birley would visit Virginia Beach, before he retired, they would sometimes have dinner with Al and Gladys at the Thunderbird. From the beginning, Al and Birley together were like Hope and Crosby. The diners around them could not help overhearing such banter as:

Birley: You're a student of the Bible, aren't you?
Al: That's right.
Birley: Well, did you know it wasn't the apple in the garden of Eden that started the trouble?
Al: Well, if it wasn't the apple, what was it?
Birley: It was the green pair (pear)!

Their combined laughter would startle even the waiters.

Al: Now, let me ask you: If the devil lost his tail, how would he get it back?

Birley: Ok, you tell me: how would he get his tail back?

Al: At a store where they re-tail spirits!

Before the chuckles died, they were off again.

Birley: I don't go for gossip, but did you hear about the fellow keeping company with a couple of school teachers?

Al: What about them?

Birley: One had a lot of class, but the other had no principles!

Charlotte and Gladys would join in the laughter and the groans when the puns were particularly atrocious.

Al's years of studying it had left him with an excellent knowledge of the Bible which was evident in his research, in his articles, and in the regular noon meditations he often led at Headquarters when he was able to get around.

Sometimes, though, when a discussion seemed overcrowded with Biblical verses and unduly technical or serious, Al could no more repress a humorous outburst than a boy with a pin could keep it away from a fat red balloon. He was fond of quoting:

> King Solomon and King David
> Lived very merry lives
> With lots and lots of lady friends,
> And many, many wives
>
> But when old age upon them crept,
> With quaking and with qualms
> King Solomon wrote the Proverbs,
> And King David wrote the Psalms.

—Adapted from *Ancient Authors*, by James Ball Naylor

The atmosphere in the A.R.E. Headquarters occasionally seemed overcharged with righteousness. Aware of his own fallibility, Al was delighted to discover an anonymous essay which seemed the perfect antidote:

What Is Heaven?

Of course you expect to go to heaven when you die . . . Take my advice. Make a reservation . . . You will want to meet your father and mother; they will be with their fathers and mothers, and their parents' parents would want to be with their parents, and so on. So you will have to meet them all. You cannot be snooty in heaven, you know. Now if you take 20 years as a generation, we find there have been 98 generations since the time of Christ. If we count only your parents and their parents and so on backwards, we find you will have to meet 302,231,454,803,657,295,676,543 different relatives.

St. John records the limits of heaven in Revelation 21:16: "He measured the city with a reed, twelve thousand furlongs. The length, the breadth and the height of it are all equal." This would equal 496,793,028,000,000,000,000 cubic feet—or 679,388,800,000,000,000 persons if packed in tight. It is apparent that heaven is filled up and was packed several hundred years ago. Obviously there is but one way out.

You must die sometime, and since it is evident you cannot go to heaven, where should you go?—You said it, not I.

With just the barest smile, Al distributed copies of the essay with its irreverent statistics around the rooms and offices of Headquarters.

Not because he was irreverent (in fact, a more reverent belief than Al's would be hard to find) but because the glad feelings inside him were like the yeast in beer, bringing up bright tangy bubbles in unplanned patterns, Al seemed irrepressible. Most of those at A.R.E. understood and empathized; only a few failed to see beyond the levity.

Back at Glad Niche, in a prominent place in the little house was hung the verse from I Samuel 25:6, "Peace be both to thee and peace be to thine house, and peace be unto all thou hast."

For a time Al had lost touch with his sister Ruth, who had gone through a divorce and a nervous breakdown. When he learned she was in St. Elizabeth's Hospital in Washington, he spoke with Gladys about his wish to help in some practical way. "Of course," Gladys had replied, and they arranged to bring Ruth to visit them at the little lakeside cottage for two weeks each summer. Ruth, who had felt anonymous in the institution and long since given up her art, now surrounded by gentleness and love, began to paint again. She worked towards recalling the skills she had developed when studying art in Paris. She left a fresh painting with Al and Gladys after each visit; one was a shimmering impression of Al among the flowers in the greenhouse.

There were some friends who confessed to visiting the cottage just to have a little of its glad atmosphere rub off on them!

One warm and welcome visitor was Kelly Freas, an artist noted especially for his unique illustrations for science fiction. Kelly also sensed the atmosphere. He did a pastel portrait of Al which—more than any photograph—seemed to glow with inner laughter.

The motto on the entrance wall was never more appropriate:

"This is the day that the Lord hath made.
Let us be glad and rejoice in it."
Psalm 118:24.

XIII
Writing and Righting

Al was never to regain all his physical vigor. But whether it was the glad atmosphere in their home, or the depth in his meditations or the mutual experiences as he often led the noon meditations at ARE Headquarters—or all of these—he became aware of a spiritual vigor which, oddly enough, seemed to grow as it was used. His outreach was wider and more sensitive, his thoughts came faster, his researches and studies fell more quickly into place with less strain than before.

After one noontime meditation, a man in his fifties came up to Al with tears in his eyes. "What you said has moved me so deeply," he said, "it means so much. Please take this," and he pressed a silver clip into Al's hand. Al did not want to take it but the look in the man's face silenced his protests. He accepted it humbly, with "Thank you and bless you."

Later, when talking about people who wanted to give, he told his niece of an elderly man who offered him a rare and beautiful plant. "That's too fine a plant for me," he had said, and refused to take it, feeling he did not deserve it. Not long afterwards, the man died. "I realized that by not accepting it, I had denied him something he really wanted to do, I had denied him the pleasure of presenting the plant," Al admitted. "It is more blessed to give than to receive, so when it will really help somebody to give, we should accept it gratefully." It was true; by accepting something sincerely offered, we would enable the giver to be "more blessed."

By midsummer, Al had completed an eight-page article, "Cry Not 'Peace, Peace' . . . ", which became the feature of the September, 1962, *Searchlight*. Based on the Edgar Cayce readings for the achievement of the new order of peace in the world, it drew its title from Reading 694–2: "Cry not 'Peace, Peace' when thou, thyself, hast not shown peace to thy brethren!" (The Biblical antecedent appears to be Jeremiah 6:14 and 8:11: "And yet they try to heal the wound of the daughter of my people mockingly, saying 'Peace, Peace' when there is no peace.") In his article Al emphasized his belief that it would be "the *living* of Christ's teachings which will save the world, rather than the attack, even on a basis of nonviolence, upon the things which make for war. For the stopping of nuclear testing will not stop the cause of war, which is fear and hatred within the human heart."

After reading this article, and knowing of Al's growing correspondence with friends and legislators, prisoners and civic leaders, his niece asked, "When you're still not back to normal, when you have to do things more slowly, how do you manage to do so much?"

It was love that helped him do it, Al answered, "I have the most beautiful example of love with me: Gladys."

Because she had been the key to his own reawakening, it followed naturally that, whatever else Al wrote about, he had to write about Gladys. He wanted to make this the best writing he could, to have the widest circulation so that others could know her too. To *The Readers' Digest* he wrote:

MY MOST UNFORGETTABLE CHARACTER

Gladys Davis blazed a trail for psychic phenomena research unparalleled in American history. There have been clairvoyants and seers in the past, but who thought to record (with a few exceptions such as Jacob Boehme and Andrew Jackson Davis) their words? Gladys Davis did just that (by sitting at the side of sleeping Edgar Cayce and recording what he said, for 22 years). She blazed this trail when the word "psychic" was sort of a "bad" word, not used in polite conversation, frowned on by most.

Rich and poor, psychiatrists, psychologists, prominent authors, physicians, ministers, priests, osteopaths, chiropractors, the sick and the well, researchers in all walks of life have daily knocked on Gladys's door since 1923. These calls are in addition to the actual work of recording the material from the unconscious mind and from the questioners. For forty-two years Gladys has been always available, to help the helpless and the helpers.

Gladys Davis is still today in Virginia Beach, quietly processing these Edgar Cayce readings which tell of the creation of the earth, prophecy of things to come, development of the soul and spirit, mind and body. She is line upon line, day by day, through her work helping people to understand themselves. Some feel that the culmination of her work on the readings of Edgar Cayce could lead to a new age, the age of enlightenmnet, the age of peace, a peace which the power of might has not brought.

To give oneself to a cause which appeals to most, such as medical or evangelical or community welfare, is certainly an admirable devotion. However, to concentrate all one's life . . . to a cause which was almost universally unpopular . . . without hope of reward, even not knowing often where the next meal was coming from, is either asinine or Christlike. . . . I first met Gladys Davis in January, 1950. At this time . . . she was earning . . . $100 a month (when sufficient contributions came in) and sending a part of this for her mother's support in Alabama. Yet I never met a happier person. . . . Accustomed as I was to Wall Street, and seekers of material wealth, it seemed to me that Gladys had more of the real gold, pure gold, spiritual gold, than all the people I had ever met combined!

He wrote about Gladys's life and work with the Cayce readings, much of which was later recorded in Mary Ellen Carter's 1972 book, updated and reissued in 1985 as *Miss Gladys and the Edgar Cayce Legacy*.

"Of many people we can say they are kind and thoughtful, and we can detail beautiful experiences exemplifying this. But Gladys, as anyone who knows her can tell you, has *all* the fruits of the spirit. . . . How do I know? On July 20, 1952, I married her. She is now Gladys Davis Turner."

The article concluded with a poem written for Gladys in 1934 by Thomas Sugrue, who wrote the first well-known book on Edgar Cayce's life, *There Is A River: The Story of Edgar Cayce*.

FOR GLADYS: AT TWENTY-NINE

How sweet to be just twenty-nine!
The grapes of youth have turned to wine,
And nature's finished her design
(All except the valentine).
The sun is used to kissing you,
And lots of men are waiting to.
Every violet knows your laughter;
Mice adore you from the rafter.
Everybody tells each other;
Mouse tells man and man tells brother;
Trees tell roots and roots tell earth:
Just how much they think you're worth.
And the price is very odd
(For who can value things of God?)
"Gladys: Made of solid gold;

> "Keep until she's very old.
> "Use with caution; do not waste;
> "Rare: Can never be replaced."
>
> —Tom Sugrue

The envelope came back from *The Readers' Digest* thick and heavy. Every page of his manuscript was inside. Plus a personal note: they truly appreciated his sharing this with them but could not see their way clear to using it.

At least, Al thought as he watched Gladys going to the door to welcome a visitor, he *had* put it down on paper. From childhood, he had wanted to let others know his thoughts but it had not been easy. Yet his father's writing was held almost in awe by friends and family. Most of Al's attempts at writing, however, had ended up as drafts for speeches, perhaps on the Red Cross circuit, or for the YMCA or his Bible classes.

After becoming acquainted with the Cayce readings, he'd had new motivation to express those thoughts. Gladys helped fire his enthusiasm, encouraged his writing, and even took time from her other activities to type his final drafts for publication. (Gladys's own background with the ARE included not only public appearances and talks but a number of articles as well.)

Other *Searchlight* articles Al wrote included "A Study of Color: The Interrelationship of Color to All Things, and Its Practical Application to the Welfare of Humanity, from the Edgar Cayce Readings," which was published in two parts (Part I, August 1963; Part II, November 1963), and an article titled "Is Reincarnation in the Bible?" He felt certain that reincarnation was a necessary ladder for the soul trying to climb closer to the Creator, and was determined not to leave this incarnation until he had been able to show in more ways the love that was growing inside him. In this article something—perhaps Al's Haitian experience—brought him to a passionate denial that belief alone could bring one to Heaven:

> No more devout believers can be found in all Christendom than those in many tropical climates and Europe who are noted for their piety *and* their propensity to steal on the way home from church, even some living as bandits and murderers; yet noted for strict observance of all the forms of the church, and for their belief in Christ! Is it possible to

believe that Jesus summarized all the virtues in one word: *belief?* If that be true, there would be no reason for His coming. . . . Is it sensible to believe that Jesus contradicted all His pronouncements on the values of piety and moral life . . . by stating . . . it was all right to believe and sin all you want? Yet this is actually what many people think!

As Jesus said, "Be ye therefore perfect, as your Father which is in Heaven is perfect." Can you mix oil and water? Should not things to be mixed be like unto one another? . . . We need to be "like" Jesus, to become one with Him, do we not? . . .

Some people think that saying a word, just a tiny work, like "believe" or "abracadabra" will open the gates of Heaven and make physical death the doorway to eternal life without ever having to abide by the Biblical truths! These people should be asked to prove that reincarnation is not. All who tap their own individual sources of eternal truths know, and do not have to prove to themselves what a truth is. The very fact that a person challenges reincarnation in the Bible indicates that person's desire for an easier way. For reincarnation is *not* an easy way.

Tapping away at his typewriter in the "chicken coop," when he came to a pause between pages or an interval between readings researches, Al would often slide over to his cot and lie down. He had to conserve his strength; there was not as much as there had been.

It seemed, though, that whenever there was a task which needed a concentration of energy, he would have the energy sufficient for the task. Whenever he felt he could help a friend, he would dredge up the strength from somewhere.

One dark summer night, well after midnight, there was a knock at the side door of the cottage. His niece, who had been visiting, was sleeping in the guest room at Glad Niche; she heard the knock, threw on a robe and opened the door. There were three young people in their teens, one a friend's daughter, who explained they had been so wrapped up in talking and singing folksongs down town they had forgotten the time. Now, all the buses to the distant area where they were staying had stopped running. Would she mind—? Doris agreed to drive them there IF she could find the way.

In moments, the sound of shuffling and the tap of a cane, and Al's sleepy voice: "What is the problem?" Al, it turned out, was the only one really familiar with the area in which they were staying, and rather than give directions, he insisted on going with them to be sure they reached their house safely. Not a word of reprimand or protest, but a matter-of-fact statement that he could help and he would.

Besides the typing and researching he did at Headquarters, Al carried on a wide and varied correspondence, with friends, with family, with anybody he thought he could help. Was he told that Peter or Jim or Mike had been sent to jail, however justly? Al would correspond regularly, letters with hope based on some of his own experiences. (Even during his last illness in 1968 he wrote a long and moving letter to a prisoner, apologizing for not being able to visit him!)

His nephew and namesake, Brinkley's oldest son, Albert E. Turner III, was having severe difficulties in his marriage in 1964. Al wrote him regularly, neither to advise nor criticize, but to "offer friendship, for that is one of the most necessary things I found when in need that fills the soul." To his niece he added,

> . . . the troubles that a person is given by the Lords of Karma are in direct ratio to his ability to bear these. The turmoil . . . is so very great that it indicates somewhat his own greatness. (The 'lukewarm' in the Book of Revelation, who are spewn out,' are those who have little either way in their goings and comings regarding emotional turmoil; the fact that a huge cross is to be borne indicates a huge person, spiritually!)
>
> What i am trying to say—the word 'Mahatma' (of course Maha = great, atman = soul) describes Al for he is a very great soul and i was hoping you might get this over to him for if he realizes this even subconsciously it will help him over the hurdles. . . . What i am praying for: not that they should be or do this or that, or, this or that happen, but that God's will be done in and through me to help them in whatever is best for their own soul development. No one except those concerned can know that which they endure to reach a higher level, and even those concerned cannot know the best solution. Only God knows this, as illustrated in the 'Gita: "Only the Knower knows," and i know that God's will will be done.

Occasionally Al would write a letter strongly urging recognition for someone he admired. In January of 1964, he wrote to the Chairman of the First Citizen Committee, which was to select the First Citizen of Virginia Beach:

> "Never having known anyone so dedicated to helping others as Hugh Lynn Cayce, I am submitting his name as First Citizen of Virginia Beach. Here are a few reasons: . . ."

He proceeded to list, in nine detailed paragraphs, Hugh Lynn's qualifications for greatness, finishing with what was to Al the most powerful one:

> "He truly lives the Sermon on the Mount in the Bible, given us by Jesus. There is hardly a person in Virginia Beach, either from youth or from church work or from many other ways, who has not been affected for good, directly or indirectly, by HUGH LYNN CAYCE."

Al was delighted to hear that Hugh Lynn would indeed receive that honor. Ironically, on the night of its presentation, Gladys and Al could not attend the dinner because Gladys was ill.

It did not always take a letter to get something done. Al's circle of friends and acquaintances was now so wide, and his familiarity with each one's needs and abilities so accurate, that it became like a hobby for him to help them fill each other's needs! At their favorite restaurant, Al asked their waitress why she seemed a bit sad. She then confided to Al and Gladys that her boyfriend had lost his job. A couple of weeks later, Doris was with them at the restaurant when the waitress spotted them and hurried over.

"Thank you for talking to that man, Mr. Turner! Joe went to see him, like you suggested, and now he has a job that's better than the old one. You are truly a saint!" Al was embarrassed but rejoiced with her; he and Gladys were especially delighted to hear that a wedding date had now been set!

A friend who had been crippled and needed help getting around was put in touch with another friend who could drive but was depressed and in need of activity. A young Quaker friend, confused about his life goals, was put in touch with Howard Brinton, the Friend whose rich philosophy had helped Al. Like the hub of a wagon wheel, Al did not have to move much to help those around him—he just had to be strongly centered.

Even when special friends moved to a great distance, Al kept in close touch. One such friend of Al and Gladys was Violet Landis, who after visiting for some months, in 1964 returned to her home in Portland, Oregon, a continent away. Al's letters to Violet revealed a many-leveled understanding between them.

When Violet wrote, regretting she was no longer a resident of Virginia Beach, he reassured her,

Truly you *are* a resident of Virginia Beach, not just *were*. For the vibrations of your love rest all through the headquarters building. . . . Surely the fine folk who *are* in Virginia Beach were with you in many incarnations, which no doubt explains your innate desire to be here, and *all* will be looking forward to when you can be here again physically, for spiritually you are always here.

At Christmastime,

The box containing the holly arrived from you Saturday. It arrived in perfect condition, protected by the love you sent with it! Bless you, dear Violet.

Only a very, very few berries dropped off, and we put these where they also could enjoy life and blessing.

The holly we put all over the house and it is decorating us beautifully for the CHRISTMAS season. i have never seen more beautiful holly, nor this particular kind which is a magnificent specimen. Thank you so very very much.

May the Christ Consciousness shine on you, dear one, this Blessed Christmas season and Gladys and i both send you our dearest love.

       Agape,
       albert

In the winter of 1964–65, when Oregon was ravaged by floods, Al and Gladys put the flood victims and Violet on their emergency prayer list. The following March, Al wrote that he would be making up his hourly prayer list again soon, and wondered if she would want to be kept on the list. He added, "The 281–5 series (of Edgar Cayce readings on prayer for others) says the asking is important so i do not want to pray for you unless you wish me to, in my hourly periods."

Perhaps as a side benefit, he added, "Would you like me also to put your home and its proper future on my prayer list? i did this with one person the other day—the next day it was sold!"

Al often expressed his belief that friends could be spiritually, telepathically in touch. He urged Violet, "Keep the 11:00 P.M. Portland time meditation as we feel togetherness and goodness then. i also can tune in better some times than others."

He did not complain in the letters of his physical condition, mentioning a handicap only when some point was to be made from it, perhaps a bond of empathy for someone who had suffered the same. He had had a bad fall in late 1966. When Violet wrote her concern, he responded with the kind of answer which seemed almost to have its own smile: "My health, after apple diet, four colonics, three steam baths, three bubble baths, four osteopathic treatments, etc., during this year so far (January 23) has overcome the fall . . . which knocked me out, but the above 'knocked me in' again and am perfectly ok. Sorry i worried you for it was temporary. Am glad your car is ok, i meant to say, i had the same experience; my vision is backwards. i see left sometimes instead of right, so quit driving."

Gladness was at the core of his correspondence, even when writing of the death of a friend:

2/9/66

"Dear Violet—Malcom passed over 5 A.M. BUT we rejoice at his spiritual Birth, he is happy—he went over happily, he saw and read over Carver booklet before going.
Blessings Light & Love
albert"

Al also wrote actively to and for the Quaker group working against capital punishment, and wrote to state legislators and any who might lend strength to this cause. His belief was that a man's life is a precious gift from God, and as long as he has it a man can grow spiritually, even in prison. To one young man, jailed at seventeen, he wrote:

Dear E———:

You may be wondering why i haven't shown up in person? Healthwise it is impossible; but the next best thing, i asked Ed Lindsley to come see you but they wouldn't let him in. He brought fruit. Did you get it? He left it for you.

You have been hourly in my prayers. Prayers are always answered. But they may be delayed. Prayers are always a two-way street. 50% depends upon the prayee, the one prayed for, the receiver, who can delay . . . by not receiving. So receive, because love is being sent you constantly.

You may have the idea that being where you are is a blot or something? It is not. Nothing, as the Daily Word sent you yesterday said, can delay the man who opens himself to his Godself within, no matter what.

In my opinion, the greatest Christian of our time was Albert Schweitzer. [At] 17 he was in jail two years, unjustly too.

The second greatest in my opinion is Kagawa, who Christianized

Japan. He spent a good deal of his earlier life in prison!

The greatest intellect of our time in my opinion was Aurobindo, a Hindu, who at 17 and 18 spent [time] in jail! The *N.Y. Times* called him this also.

Starr Daily you know, living today, spent much of his youth in prison: many prisoners like this have done much to help those in prison and out.

i am told St. Francis of Assisi spent his late teens in prison!

Not that i can be compared with these, but at 17 i was in jail! And i am not sorry, it was a great experience! To me there can be no finer place to be than in jail. After all, our *only* purpose in living, in coming into this incarnation, our only purpose is to help others. We must go from here to there and everywhere to find people to help. BUT in jail, one doesn't have to go anywhere. They are all there, as many as one wants to, they are there, wanting to be helped, waiting to be helped, crying to be helped, and YOU ARE THERE, able and willing to help them. It is a great privilege to be in jail, one of the greatest. After all, the foundation of the Christian church was started when St. Paul was in jail more than once. And remember Tolstoy, who inspired Mahatma Gandhi to free India by nonviolence? Remember Henry Thoreau was in jail when Ralph Waldo Emerson came by and said, surprised, "What are you doing in there, Henry?" and Thoreau answered, "What are you doing *out* there, Waldo?"

EVERYONE is where they are for a purpose! All those people above were in for the purpose of helping others. Kagawa wrote a most stirring book, *Love, the Law of Life,* and tells of how he lost an eye in jail when he helped another and got infected, and thanked God for loss of an eye—He could help others more because of it.

Everyone, i repeat, is where they are for a reason, and by the grace of God. You are, i am, Mother is, everyone is, at a place because that *is* the best place they can help others.

Everyone in the Meeting who knows where you are, i am certain, is praying for you. NO ONE condemns you. Even Jesus has forgiven you already. Only one person remains to forgive you and this is YOURSELF. When you can forgive yourself whatever it is you feel you need to forgive yourself for, then the PRISON door, like for St. Paul, will open. Prison, after all, like anything else, is only for a lesson. When the lesson is learned, there is no longer any need for the prison. After all, the body is a prison, everything is a prison IF one considers it such. BUT wherever you are, i am, anyone is, IS an opportunity, and when one can turn stumbling blocks into stepping stones, (he) can turn so-called misfortunes into opportunities. Then one is FREED, for self is the only one who can imprison. Please take the opportunities of helping the many over there; they need you, desperately. You know so much more than they do. We, all of us, have to take advantage of ALL opportunities, else we have to come back life after life, life after life, and meet the same opportunities over again. Prison is the best opportunity there is to help other people. i *know* you will get great gain, more than any money or price from where you are, and help many. My prayers are with you. Please take them.

      Very, very sincerely,
        albert

Al knew very well, by now, that "the body is a prison" and that "everything is a prison IF one considers it such." Unlike Jack London's "Star Rover," who had out-of-body experiences while confined to a cell, Al was learning while within his infirm body how great a stretch of mental and sprititual freedom there could be.

XIV

Revealing the Revelation

It was in late summer, 1962, that they came to him as he sat at his desk in the "chicken coop," and asked how he was doing. They wondered if he would feel up to it. After all, they had enjoyed the previous ones so much! Would Al, could he, consider taking and teaching another class on Revelation? (Since he had first begun teaching a class in Revelation at ARE Headquarters in 1953, some months after he and Gladys were married, he had managed to be there every week, except for the times he was in the hospital or simply unable to walk. He had enjoyed the classes, and they had enjoyed him! Of course, this last attack and stroke had been so severe that those who listened to the doctors hadn't even expected Al to leave his home, so they had almost given up.)

Something in Al stirred strongly.

The doctors had given orders not to strain, to nap often, but then the doctors also thought he would be always in a wheelchair.

At home Al discussed it with Gladys. "I think I can. I'd like to try it."

After a moment Gladys asked, "But can you do it on your own? Going into the class, getting your material and references together, everything that's involved?" Every day Gladys was driving Al with her to ARE Headquarters and seeing that he went safely down to his little office as she went over to hers. And she didn't worry as long as he stayed in that one place, with a cot and blanket next to the desk for easy resting. (Gladys's work involved the letters and readings no one else could handle, the original papers and the readings with the actual names of the people involved. Gladys it was who transformed the names in the originals to the numbers on the transcripts as she typed and indexed the remaining readings for use in the library and publications. The office staff cooperated actively in protecting Gladys, screening her calls, fending off interruptions. Gladys was just not available for casual things; it was understood.)

Al closed his eyes and drew a breath, then opened them and smiled. "It will be fine. They will share their energy with me."

AFTER LEADING A NOONTIME MEDITATION, in fall of 1967, Albert paused outside of A.R.E. Headquarters to share some happiness with a friend.

Gladys worried. "You know you're not supposed to overdo."
Al shook his head, grinning. "I'm afraid I'll underdo!"
And so it would continue. A room was set aside for the Revelation class; the word went out, and on the agreed-on day at ten Al made his way there with the aid of his cane, while cautious class members stayed near. Applause and laughter greeted him as he entered.
This was what he truly enjoyed, tossing challenges to his friends and those who would soon become his friends, challenges to the re-

alization of attunement, the realization of at-one-ment, along the steps that were buttressed by the Cayce readings on the Book of Revelation, and Al's other studies on it.

Despite the extra effort, it was as Al had hoped: there was more energy flowing to him from the people in the class. He could feel it! It was still a struggle to take care of the many tasks he had set himself but it seemed less of a struggle now that his beloved Revelation group was going again.

It seemed that in this group he was sharing concepts from his own life's search, a search that had begun eons ago when a twelve-year-old boy climbed attic stairs looking for a miracle. Every year had added more pieces to the puzzle.

Back in 1957, in fact, he had prepared a manuscript on "The Revelation Decoded," based on his studies and research for his teaching the St. Luke's Bible Class in the 1940's. This included the readings of Edgar Cayce on Revelation, and material from James M. Pryse's book *The Apocalypse Unsealed*. Al's manuscript was not, however, accepted by the A.R.E. Press for publication; one reviewer felt it had too much of the esoteric.

In his preface to "The Revelation Decoded," Al had expressed his own feelings: "The meaning of the Revelation of St. John the Divine has been so distorted by translators from the beginning of the Christian era that it has become absolutely meaningless from the exoteric (outer or popular) point of view. [It] . . . however, can become perfectly clear to anyone whose mind is open to esoteric or spiritual inner meanings."

A special eloquence, a special fervor, came to Al as he led these discussions. They were, indeed, anything but traditional. Although at first they might seem conventional to a visitor, very shortly the range of topic, depth, and spontaneous additions would have the listeners riveted. [Thanks to Violet Landis, who taped some of the 1967 classes, we have been able to hear several of them, and can offer some excerpts which seem to be typical of Al in action.]

At the opening of one class, Al explained: "We have a different kind of meditation, which we've developed over thirteen years. We generally read a psalm (I think today it's the 70th) and then we'll have a period of silence, then the Lord's Prayer, then an affirmation. It's coming to me very strongly that there is an affirmation from the Edgar Cayce readings that we might adopt as a permanent affirmation. Is that all right?

"'There is that consciousness in me' (that's the Christ-consciousness) 'that is sufficient for every need within my body, mind and soul.'" Everyone repeated it together.

"I thought it would be a good idea to begin at the beginning . . . with the readings . . . In 1930 a young girl had a reading and . . . the doctor was told to read Gray's *Anatomy* alongside of the Book of Revelation. In 1933, this prayer group, part of Study Group Number 1, arranged a forum on the Book of Revelation with questions for Edgar Cayce. This began with the reading known as #281–16, given to the prayer group, and all the Revelation readings are part of the prayer group reading.

"Actually, the name of the book isn't even Revelation! The earliest available manuscripts carried the title in Greek, *Epopteia. Apokalypsis,* 'unveiling' or "revelation" was a later word. *Epopteia* means 'initiation' . . . so in effect this book is a book of an initiation of selfhood into Godhood. And as a 'Book of Initiation,' what is revealed in it could only be revealed by a translation of the symbols."

"But," someone asks, "aren't symbols abstract?"

"This is an abstract thing, you say. It's very fine and I believe it but—how is it practical?" Al went on.

"Well, if you take problems—I've never met anybody that didn't have problems—problems all come from conflict. All of them. Including my own or anybody's. They come from conflict in the soul.

"And there are four types of conflict. We can take these as the four horsemen [of the Apocalypse, of Revelation]. We have on the one side: poverty, ignorance, bigotry and disease; we have on the other side: love, joy, peace and compassion. They're the same thing—the same horsemen! After all, a mounted horseman, in the Greek, is the same thing as 'angel'—they're both messengers!

"So these horsemen are riding down to the four horsemen within us in the four lower glands [Al had named them from the readings earlier]. We're dealing with 'em every time we *think!* And each of us has at least 500,000 thoughts a day! Now, if we take these four horsemen, and they're going this way and that way at the same time, here's what happens: There's a conflict between *reason* and *passion.* There's a conflict between *desire* and *conscience.* There's a conflict between *good* and *evil.* There's a conflict between *spirit* and *flesh.* They are four different horsemen.

"You want to solve these problems? It's very simple. That's what we're going to do in this *Revelation* thing. We take these symbols from the *Book of Revelation* and make them practically applicable. Every conflict that you face, or every problem—if we jast take those four things, concentrate on the positives instead of the other four negatives—these are four conflict areas: good and evil, reason and passion, desire and conscience, spirit and flesh. Problems in these areas solve themselves if you pick the positives, through the *Book of Revelation* material. There's a definite pathway through the four lower glands of the centers. We need to follow it to completely conquer the lower nature that has its seat in those centers.

"Now, we have a choice: good and evil, flesh and spirit—nobody's compelling us, we have free will. But if we would rather fall into a ditch, it is a free choice. Or we can have this (protective) wall around us; if we're living within spiritual law, then nothing can happen to (really harm) us anywhere, but if we're living outside spiritual law, everything can happen to us everywhere.

"So, if we want to live within that law, or wall, whatever you want to call it, we need this *Book of Revelation* because it will teach us how we can conquer these four lower life centers. I don't care who you are, or where in the world you are, to conquer these four lower centers there's no better outline in the whole world than the *Book of Revelation*."

"Will that lead us towards salvation?"

"When asked, 'What is salvation?' the reading answered, 'You can only be saved from self. There is no other salvation.' We are, then, to be saved from self and from getting into a mess and falling into a ditch." Al's voice rose to a brief crescendo. "IF WE SO CHOOSE, we can fall in the ditch and God doesn't do anything about it. He leaves us free will, and if he prevented us from falling in the ditch he would take away from us that free will. We need that falling into the ditch. We do it" (here he speeded his words) "again, again, again, again, again—SO WE LEARN! that this salvation is a saving from self.

"When we are saved from self, it is an arduous process, not of an evangelistic, temporary emotional mood, by the statement of a word, but of a pathway of centuries, nay of milleniums of effort, unremitting effort. And that's what we're in this for. We wouldn't be here unless we were.

"So if there are no questions, we might as well start at 281–16."

Used as a text was the *Commentary on the Book of THE REVELATION"*, material based on a study of Twenty-Four Psychic Discourses by Edgar Cayce, compiled by efforts of a Study Group with editing by Esther Wynne.

Interspersed with the readings and commentary, Al would offer congratulations on someone's birthday, on another class member's health food store, add encouragement and jokes. Then they would get back to a subject like *Salvation*.

"Manly Hall, one time, said the path of salvation is trod only by those who have a practical, scientific knowledge of the occult functions of the body."

(It is impossible, with mere print, to give the effect of Al's rich voice, its almost musical fluctuations in tone and rhythm, which somehow seemed to bring complete thoughts even from incomplete sentences. He was trying the near impossible, seeking terms to compare spiritual with physical ecstasy, to share the indescribable joy he had been able to experience even after his stroke, the tremendous thrill of finding the Christ-consciousness within, the Light within. It was a uniting of God-given elements, Al believed, that brought forth this Light. How could he explain it in ordinary words, compare it to ordinary experiences? What common experience did people tend to idealize? It helps to realize that he was trying, with ordinary words, to describe concepts that reached beyond words, seeking terms to compare religious with physical ecstasy, spiritual with physical light. For many in the class, he succeeded.)

"We learn, as we study the occult functions, that sex is the principle creative activity. Now, if we look at it, we see we are born, and from the first instant of a cry, or the change of diapers, the attitude of man or woman is the same: 'Look! Look at me!'—to be recognized, and let the ego push out, until a certain age . . . when the ego starts to submerge itself. . . 'Then shall the King say unto those who are on the right hand, enter ye into the realm of the blessed, for inasmuch as ye have done it unto the least of these ye have done it unto me.' Then the cells come in and unite, for in each of us are both, for each woman has the male, each man has the female, they unite . . .

"And in the first book of John, where it says there are three who bear witness, the spirit, the water and the blood, and these three are one (John I. 5:8), the water is the creative function of the sperm cells. The spirit is the kundalini (Hindu term for life force) and the blood— is the blood. They combine, and ignite, become on fire. (The enthusiasm in his voice seemed itself ablaze.) They must be raised in a life tome of service to glory. When they unite, we are married [within ourselves]." The uniting of male-female forces in creative energy was as the marriage of the Lamb.

Leading the group towards an emotional comparison, Al continued, "No soul is ever lost, but it loses its way. The higher part, or the spirit, is split off. And there is this unremitting, tireless effort of the soul to find itself. Not to find some guy out in space, some four of five million miles out there, but *itself*!" He likened the reuniting of the parts of the soul with the uniting of man and woman: "You wanted to know what God-realization was. There is an experience between man and woman, the highest experience on the physical plane, when we feel the closest to God, but this is the lowest of the four planes of existence. This is where creation takes place, when the creative cells in both of us, man and woman, turn inward and re-create. How is this done? Through meditation, slowly and increasing, as when we focus our mind upon the one thought, we actually become that thought.

"Every religion in the world has basically its symbols in nature, in the occult functions of the body as related to the macrocosm. Having on the lowest plane of existence the greatest sex experience, or union between man and woman, we experience a *moment* of ecstasy. On the other hand, if this marriage between the bride and the Lamb is happening within ourselves, this experience is not for an *instant* but is for *all eternity*! You are always lifted up, in that ecstatic frame of mind! (Those of you who have seen Dr. Lander speak know he is a good example of this: he's just not there! He's so lifted up!) And this is true of many others. As the union of the sperm and the ovum occurs within the androgyous part of ourselves, we become one. We have that experience, the greatest treasure in the world. Then the prodigal son (that's you and me) says, 'I will return to my father!' and the return is complete.

"Now this isn't something five million years from now, or tomorrow or any other day, it's right now that we have this experience. And we can have euphoria, religious ecstasy or whatever you want. The experience will occur at any time the individual so wills it."

Harry spoke up, worried that this experience did not seem a suitable goal. "It sounds like a lot of this was in Hinduism."

"No," Al protested, "No, because this is when Jesus went about *doing good*. Most of us just go about." The euphoria was real—but there was much more than just feeling.

Harry objected, "He didn't expand his consciousness along with it."

Al replied, "This is what I'm getting at. You cannot expand your consciousness without going about just as Jesus did, being of service. For 'Glory,' say the readings, 'means service.'" His voice, full of emotion, then softened and there was a moment of silence.

As the class would continue with the questions and answers from the readings of the Revelation (281 series), a member would often come up with a spontaneous comment that would lead to another branch of discussion.

One woman, with a little laugh, began, "Something funny happened last night. I don't know whether I should have asked for it or not. I wanted to be one with Christ last night. One with Him. So when I was going to sleep, that's what I asked." She laughed self-consciously. "Something kept waking me up! It was really rough."

The group appeared to realize she had had a spiritual but puzzling experience. When Al continued he focused on what he saw as the root of her discomfort: the sleeping problem. "Now, at the beginning of the class," he explained to her, "we talked about breathing. This is more powerful than any pill that's given, like any sleeping pill or whatever: proper breathing. And by proper breathing—it's an individual thing. We've got to get all the bad air out of the lungs, so in comes the good. We've got to inhale deeply, get all the air in and fill the lungs, and then exhale. This is an individual matter but it's got to be in rhythm and it's got to be a deep breathing. If we go 'uh–uh–uh' (Al demonstrated shallow breathing), this shortens one's life, and also the blood cells of the body don't have the chance to transform into light—which they must do.

"There is a book called *Bio-Pneuma*, which is written by Levi, the author of *The Aquarian Gospel of Jesus the Christ*. A small book, it's in the locker, upstairs. The most important factor probably in all our life is *breathing*. It's difficult, not only to give a chant, which we do in this group, but to have a good meditation, with shallow breathing. (He demonstrated.) You see there's still a lot of impure matter in the inner lungs, which hasn't been cleansed.

"The readings say, again, that the will must be made one with Him, and when we breathe we can work towards this. Lou Austin has said that you can develop a way to breathe out 'love for all the world'— breathe it out to complete standstill. Then your subconscious takes over, it's automatic. But all this breathing can be multiplied in our own personal application of the divine spirit . . .

"Human spirit, which can be divided into millions or billions, reaches out for a search for God in the spirit. But the One Spirit—there's only one, as the Indians put it, Great Spirit—the individual unit, can't be divided, it is all of us. (Here his voice took on a tone near ecstasy.) And now is the accepted time, that is saying—as so many of the affirmations do— 'Now, Give me, Father, Now, Teach me, Now!'— The present time, the accepted time. And by tuning up, as in a complete symphony orchestra of the world, there isn't a possibility we can be wrong. What a beautiful opportunity!

"And it's available to all! There is no charge. It's a free gift. That is, it's a free gift but we still gotta work for it, because there's always an IF. Because it's free doesn't mean we don't pay for it. It's the heaviest cost there is. We've got to give *ourselves*. And as we give ourselves to this infinite force, we become one with the force, members one of another.

"I have talked too long. Are there any questions?"

The class, caught up with him in an entrancing dimension, would take a few moments to come back to the world of sea breezes and wooden chairs and ticking clocks.

As Al worked and prayed and took on the classes, he tried to bring the group towards an experience he was convinced of, an experience he had begun to feel was possible now, an experience that would account for this euphoric explosion of inner light he sensed and pictured.

"In the beginning there was light. 'Now,' said John, *'In Him was life, and the life was the light of men.'* Now the light came into the world and the world knew it not. The world of the senses, the world of the cells of the body, crystallized the light in the blood. And it is only Oneness that can be had, complete Oneness, by turning the blood into light! And the one, one and only, Father is that light. As we transform the blood cells into light, in meditation, as they are placed into service and glory . . . until all the blood cells turn into light . . . We are transformed. And this is what Paul meant when he said in Romans 12:2, *Be ye transformed . . .* in mind. And when we start with 'Mind is the Builder'—as we build, this water of life comes from the 'shedding' of blood. No, we don't cut ourselves and let the blood run all over the floor! It is the transformation of the blood into light!"

Again the class would continue with the Revelation readings, and again Al would offer additional Cayce readings to amplify or clarify.

One man read, "Question 27. 'Solar plexus—Debts?' and the answer is 'Yes!'" Laughter followed with kidding on the size of someone's solar plexus, and how the symbolism might apply.

Al commented, "I think that's self-explanatory, because our debts are *karma* ordered for us. What we're really talking about in the Lord's Prayer is that *karma* area. 'Forgive us our debts'—What we're saying is 'Eliminate our bad *karma*,' in effect, 'Make us worthy to overcome this bad *karma*'. This is our debt, that we've got to react to.

"It might be well, Jane, if you want to read what I've got on the 'Mind' to clarify . . . I have some readings with their numbers."

"Where did you find that?" Jane wanted to know.

"I extracted it. If you want, Jane, you can give the number."

Jane read, "1236-2, This is, 'Mind is the builder. Spirit is the light. Physical is the result.' 1246-2, see also Spirit. 'Mind: that which is the creative force, in an animate object. The thoughts are in it, of the creator. That which is the builder. And may be classified into two forces. Between the soul and physical, and that between the soul and spiritual. That factor which is in direct opposition to will. All right.'

"The next is 'The conscious mind: That which is able to be manifested in the physical plane through one of the senses. That which reasons the impressions from the senses they manifest before the individual.'

"The next is 'The subconscious mind: That line between the soul and the spirit forces, in an entity. And it is reached more thoroughly when the conscious mind is under the subjugation of the soul-forces of the individual, or physical body.'"

Al spoke up, "See, I think that's the answer there. That's what we're saying—the same thing, see? in a different way."

Jane continued, "'We see the manifestation of these in the so-called 'spiritual-minded' people. The manifestation of he subconscious in their actions, that portion of the body better known as that which propagates or takes care of the body physical, mental or what-not, when it is not able to take care of itself.

"'The subconscious is unconscious force. Its action may be brought into manifestation by the continual doing of certain acts in the physical plane. The body becomes unconscious of doing the acts that it does.

"'The next is the superconscious mind: the Divine, the Oneness, lies between soul and spirit forces within the spiritual entity. Not of the earth forces at all, only awakened with the spiritual indwelling and the quiet, individually. Mind . . . the true force . . . spiritual forces . . . within the spiritual entity, not of the earth forces at all'."

"That's got them all," Al said happily. "And there is a reading which I would like to bring in later on. I can't recall the number but it said, 'In the beginning, God created light . . .'"

As the class ended, several of the members embraced him. He loved them, and in the shared affection felt an afterglow.

XV

. . . And There Was Light

Members of the A.R.E. Prayer Group received an unusual letter the third week in June of 1968:

> Wednesday night, June 19, 1968
> General Hospital of Virginia Beach
> Intensive Care Unit

(This letter was dictated to Gladys by Albert E. Turner, admitted to the ICU from Virginia Beach Hospital Annex about 1:00 A.M. Wednesday.)

Dear Ruth and the Prayer Group:

What more propitious time to come into the hospital than the night before the Prayer Group Meeting?

Just like Tom Sugrue wrote of seeing the vignettes on the wall while he was suffering in the hospital (in his book, *Stranger in the Earth)*, here I was with my eyes closed, the clock ticking away—9:45–9:55. I always try to be in prayer in the Prayer Group a little before 10:00. So I was preparing myself to be receptive to your prayers a little before 10:00, trying to envision who was sending them out—Ruth sitting over in the north corner, and Abbie Hughes—Hugh Lynn—and sweet Olive as always—Lydia—Virginia Cooke—then perhaps one or two more of the faithful I didn't recognize. I was looking for Paul Owen, but "He isn't here yet—he will be here in a minute, I know." The clock ticks on.

I can't get out of the habit of opening the meeting, but now I know I must let somebody else do it. I can feel that something is happening. Like Tom Sugrue's account. Ten minutes after ten—something is happening.

"Albert can see it's happening!" Abbie Hughes is having something to do with this, letting it happen, and maybe Lydia too. "Albert can't help but feel it!"

I am trying to see the people who are not there backing her up, as each in the Prayer Group, through Lydia, desires that *THY WILL BE DONE—THINE!*" This is what she always emphasizes. "We ask this for Albert Turner in the Virginia Beach Hospital." I heard these words.

I *felt* the Prayer Group. Nothing like this ever happened before. We talk about the healing light. This experience was one of the darkest, physically, mentally, spiritually, that has ever happened, psychically, emotionally—and I was lifted out of it by a band of healing light shining out from you all, which I could see and feel going into me. Like a drowning man I grabbed this healing band like a life preserver.

I'm still holding onto my life preserver. I thank you, dear ones, for being this to me—and for your continued prayers on next Wednesday and the ones thereafter. I've been given an extended life line, thanks to you.

Albert

On Monday, June 24, Gladys sat at Al's bedside telling him of all the things he had done to make her happy—there were so many of them!—even his thoughtfulness in having a toilet and washbasin put in the little back room so she could have a "private bath," which for her had always been the "*nth* degree of luxury." For the years since, he had used that little room for his needs except showering. But, Gladys later wrote her brother Boyd, Al just smiled and said, "That dear Boyd did that!" (It was Boyd who, at Al's request, had fixed the room.) He kept smiling, not so much because of what Gladys said he had done to make her happy, but because she was sitting beside him.

Still, he worried a bit, thinking of things he had wanted to do but had not yet done, to help others. He wanted to write to a man in Louisville, who he thought might be a help to Gladys's nephew. There were so many things waiting.

As Gladys kissed him good night, he told her, "Take care of yourself, Beautiful!"

Early Tuesday morning, massive brain damage. He went into a coma and stayed until 9:15 Thursday evening, June 27.

Gladys recalled Al looked forward, in a sense, to death—calling it a birth. He had often laughed and said, "Everybody is joyous at birth except the baby; everybody is sad at a funeral except the deceased."

Memorial services in the Quaker tradition were held simultaneously at the Virginia Beach Friends' Meeting House and in the A.R.E. Auditorium. Around the Virginia Beach Friends' Meeting was a fragrant aura, almost a halo, of white gardenias from bushes that Al had planted years before around the meeting house. Several Friends expressed surprise: "Never knew the gardenias to be in bloom *this* early before!"

Louise Wilson, a friend of Al and Gladys, recalled that one day at Friends' meeting for worship, her husband Bob had said, "That's a pretty tie you have on, Albert!" Al took it off and gave it to Bob; Bob took his off and gave it in exchange. Al's tie had the word "love" written in tiny letters all over it. At the memorial service, Bob wore the tie, and spoke of Albert's unqualified love.

At the service, Louise's mother, Christine Brown, sat in the seat where Albert always sat. As she was sitting there, she said she was filled with the spirit, and the words she had often heard Albert say during the many times she'd been to the meeting. "She said she felt both honored and humbled to sit in his place," Louise recalled, "It was like a sacred seat."

The memorial booklet, *A Tribute to the memory of Albert E. Turner, a minister deceased, issued by the Virginia Beach Monthly Meeting of Friends, held at Virginia Beach, Virginia,* opened with a poem by an unnamed young man, which began:

> There is a river
> of which we are all part
> We are currents,
> The streams of that river.
> God flows through us,
> to be directed by our wills.
> Al Turner was a channel, a current.
> He moved the river and it flowed into me.
> Now the river has taken him
> and he has flowed into the sea . . .

The booklet offered a history of his life and service, some of his favorite phrases and sayings, such as "Faith is fear that has said its prayers," adding "He prayed so constantly that his life became a prayer."

From Virginia Beach and from across the country, people wrote to Gladys, sharing love and their appreciation of this unassuming man who had somehow managed to convince them of the rightness of "Happy Birthday!"

"His customary greeting," Olive Lander recalled, "woke everyone up to the possibility of a new and more cheerful start in whatever you were about. He was always the Santa Claus, you know, in our staff

Christmas parties, spreading good will and jollity. He is unforgettable—dear Al, always bearing cheer and a belief in the good. Wherever he went, good cheer prevailed."

"His spirit shone through his entire body like a light," another friend wrote, "It disregarded illness and trouble. It warmed everyone with whom he came in contact.

"His deep knowledge helped us over many knotty problem areas. He was never didactic, but always assumed the other knew as much as he, but might have forgotten temporarily the matter under discussion.

"It is not hyperbole for me to say that knowing Albert has been a great privilege for us; he is, probably, as close to being a saint as anyone who we expect to meet in this still imperfect world."

Accolades were good to hear. But for someone whose life had been so closely shared with another, praises were no substitute for the missing squeeze of the hand, the missing arm around the shoulder, the missing *presence*. Certainly not for Gladys.

For seven months she tried to go on as usual but found herself at times just in tears, in the car, in the office or at home—where Al had been with her so much. She had been making excuses for getting out of social activities and other meetings, "doing as little as I could, always making some excuse or other." Though Al's own cheerful words about death, and Edgar Cayce's words about "God's Other Door," were some comfort, there was still the sense of loss, of something vital missing.

"Lately," Gladys wrote her brother Boyd, "I had begun to feel that I just had to have some assurance that Al knew what I was thinking, how much I missed him, and that he was as right over there as he had thought he would be. . . . Actually, I was only half alive—such a hurt feeling inside."

Al had understood her work on the readings so well, and often had said how he wished he could help her. "Of course," Gladys said, "he did help me in so many ways. He did more research on the readings than anyone else I know, and we'd discuss his findings in the various readings as he went through the index extracting material which threw light on Bible passages, etc."

She had been dreading the coming of her birthday, January 30, because of the memories it would bring of the way Al made a festive day of it from morning till night.

On the afternoon of her birthday, working on a new Circulating File (for loan to members) that Dr. McGarey had sent from the A.R.E. Clinic in Arizona with notations on special readings he wanted included, Gladys noticed the copy he had sent of reading 1140–2 was very dim. (1140–2 would be the second reading given for a person whose name, on published readings, had been changed to 1140.) This meant she and the new typist, Patricia, would need to get out the Master Copy for retyping (as they had been doing with other readings whose Master Copies were so dim they could hardly be reproduced). She went to the cabinet and took out the proper folder, 1140, but when she checked the contents, 1140–2 was not there.

It is a very worrisome thing for a reading to be misfiled—with over 14,000 of them, it could be lost for an interminable time! (One reading had been misfiled and was not found for months.) Then the thought struck Gladys "as if someone had knocked on my head":

"Well, you took out 1040 by mistake awhile ago. Maybe somebody misfiled it in 1040."

What a long shot! Gladys thought, but went back and looked into the 1040 folder anyway. Sure enough, there next to 1040–1 was 1140–2. "We were flabbergasted," Gladys said later. Pat cheered, "Things sure are clicking for you today!"

With that reading taken care of, she went on to the next case, with reading 2434—2. This also was so dim it should be retyped. Gladys went back to the insulated file again to get the master copy. It also was missing! In all these thousands of readings, where could she begin to look? How she wished for Hugh Lynn Cayce's ability to find immediately whatever book or reference he wanted at the moment.

"As if in answer to my wish," Gladys remembers, "immediately there was that 'knock on my head' again with this thought.

'You found the other reading one hundred readings apart—why don't you look in 2334?'

"Without question I pulled out the 2330 folder and there, behind 2334–1 was 2434–2! Suddenly it was clear, pure knowledge on my part—no guessing or surmising. What better way could Al choose to demostrate, on my birthday yet, that he was aware of everything I was thinking?"

Though Gladys had been quite tired from lack of sleep the night

GLADYS DAVIS TURNER at the doorway of Glad Niche, 1984.

before, energy flowed through her now. She kept going happily till after midnight.

The next day her nephew commented, "You look ten years younger!"

"I feel it, too!" was her glad reply.

Gladys found it interesting that when she returned to church the following Sunday after a long absence, the minister's sermon topic was "The Missing Note."

She listened intently, wondering if there could be another message here. Then the minister revealed the note that was missing was

JOY

The church was filled with light.
Gladys smiled.

Appendix

REINCARNATION and ALBERT TURNER

The concept of reincarnation, of a soul returning to the earth after death to live another physical life, has existed as far back as written history, at least.

Some readers, such as those who belong to the Association for Research and Enlightenment, have access to a library with hundreds of books on the subject, but other readers may have seen only what has surfaced in the popular media, e.g. *The Search for Bridey Murphy*, by Morey Bernstein, in the early 1950's, later Dr. Gina Cerminara's *Many Mansions* and *The World Within*; the film, *The Reincarnation of Peter Proud;* recently, such books as Shirley MacLaine's Out on a Limb, W.H. Church's *Many Happy Returns*, Jess Stearn's *Soulmates*, Richard Bach's *The Bridge Across Forever,* etc.

Dr. Leslie Weatherhead, eminent British Methodist, in his book, *The Christian Agnostic,* presented some cases in the chapter "Reincarnation and Renewed Chances." Dr. Ian Stevenson, of the University of Virginia, presented research of worldwide scope in his monograph, *Twenty Cases Suggestive of Reincarnation*. Published in 1966, it is still considered one of the most—if not THE most—scholarly treatments of the subject.

Some people consider the gathering of evidence as the chief purpose of research. They are delighted when someone like Joanne McIver in Alberta, Canada, can be regressed to a life recent enough for recollections to be checked out. (Jess Stearn, *The Search for the Girl with the Blue Eyes.*)

When Al offered himself as a volunteer to Dr. Henry George in Wilmington, Delaware, he knew Dr. George was seeking evidence to be used towards proof of reincarnation. For Al, however, the main purpose of the hypnotic regressions was not to "prove" that he had been Jack Carstairs or the son of James I or Achmesh. It was rather to learn, from the previous experiences, what his soul's purpose was for this life. Was he developing as he should? How could he do better?

Although in each of the eight sessions Al was regressed to several lifetimes, here the information on a single lifetime has been kept together.

This information is presented with no claim that everything he said under hypnosis is factually accurate. Although there have been numerous cases when a hypnotized person has given information about other areas, times and places that has proved correct (not to mention the thousands of readings of Edgar Cayce that were verified), there is no guarantee that hypnotizing a man will make him speak the truth. He will speak what is in his MIND, from the state where the hypnotist has led him. For example, if Al were regressed to the age of ten, in the life of Jack Carstairs, and asked what was going on in the Civil War, he might respond with no more accuracy than the average ten-year-old.

Some inconsistencies did appear. Regressed to the age of two years, in his current life, Al gave the address of 6366 Woodbine Avenue for his home. When he was thirteen, we know it was 6435 Woodbine. He might have given the wrong address, or the family might have lived there and then moved. In the life of Jack Carstairs, he referred to his early home as being in Columbus, but in a later session as in Dayton, Ohio. There are others.

There are also errors in transcription found in the sessions where it was possible to compare the typists' work with the actual sound of the recordings. (Some wire recordings were found by serendipity among the materials in the home of a friend of Dr. George. Thanks to William Newlin's repairing an old wire recorder and transferring the material to cassettes, we were able to hear the actual voices of Albert and Dr. George for part of the second session, all of the third and part of the seventh.)

Typical clarifications:

> Typist: There was a sort of hill, I forget what in the hell, and there was a hill like in front of kind of trees."
> Recording: There was a sort of hillock, it wasn't a hill. There was a hillock in front of some kind of trees.
>
> Typist: I couldn't see this wanting murder.
> Recording: I couldn't see this wanton murder.
>
> Typist: It was a little ways away.
> Recording: It was a long ways away.

Because the transcripts appeared to be done on two different typewriters, it is assumed there were two typists. Neither one appeared familiar with the spelling of any foreign languages. In the many cases where Dr. George or another questioner would ask the hypnotized man to say a word or phrase in his "native" tongue, it was difficult to tell from the transcript what sound was actually given. For those parts which were included in the discovered wire recordings, it was possible to make close approximations, since the author is familiar with the sound of French, German, Spanish, Italian, Latin, and Greek.

With these caveats, we may look at the edited transcripts of these sessions, Al's recollections of different lives. We will find some patterns from former lives which correspond to happenings in later ones. We can be confident that these recollections were a real part of Al's total personality.

THE LIVES OF ALBERT TURNER

("Dr." refers to Henry George III, M.D., Wilmington, Delaware, physician and hypnotist. Each of the sessions was preceded by the hypnotic induction and preliminary questions. The transcripts included not only date and time but list of witnesses for each session.)

JACK CARSTAIRS (about 1845 to 1895)

Dr: And now we want you to go back before this, before you were born. We want you to go back on a trip into the past. Now you can do that. You have that power. And you go back. Go back to your first experience. Tell us where you were, who you were.
Al: I need help getting back, I can't seem to get back.
Dr: We will help you. We want you to go back, completely relax, . . . Now you will find this a very pleasant experience. You have many pleasant memories. Bring these memories up to the surface for us.
Al: Jack, that was my name, Jack.
Dr: Jack What?
Al: Can't remember.
Dr: Tell us more about Jack. You can bring it up.

Al: Carstairs. 1945.
Dr: That was when you were born. Where were you born?
Al: Columbus, Ohio. The street was 171 Jackson Avenue.
Dr: What was your father's name?
Al: Samuel
Dr: And your mother's name?
Al: Ruth
Dr: Did you have a happy home there?
Al: Very happy.
Dr: Tell us about it?
Al: There was grass. In the front yard was a tree, a maple tree.
Dr: Did you go to school there? Bring it up.
Al: School? Some kind of school. Red brick, that's all I remember. Two blocks away. Teacher there was named Gimbel, Miss Gimbel.
Dr: And what did you do when you stopped school?
Al: Eight years old, September 1, 1853. Climbing a tree and the second branch broke and I fell.
Dr: Were you hurt?
Al: Yeah, I fell about ten feet, onto the grass. On my backside. Didn't hurt too much, but I run in bawling. My father . . . put a wet cloth on my head, in the livingroom. The rug was red, it had blue spots on it, in the front room. We had horses, and there was one of them at the front door. The porch had a railing around it. . . . And my father said, 'Jack, you all right?' He was crying. I was hurt.
Dr: What did your father do?
Al: He put a wet cloth on my head. It just feels like . . . It felt good.
Dr: What was your father's occupation?
Al: He was a carpenter, told me to be a carpenter.
Dr: Did you like being a carpenter.
Al: Not particularly.
Dr: What did you want to be?
Al: Ride horses. You mean when I was eight, don't you? I wanted to go out west . . . gold rush, and everybody going out west and hitching the wagons up.
Dr: And did you go?
Al: No, I didn't go west.
Dr: How much land did your farm have?

Al: Ten acres.
Dr: Did you have a wood lot? Were there trees growing on it?
Al: Let me see, yeah. Over there was sort of a hillock, it wasn't a hill, and there was a hillock in front with some kind of trees, I didn't know what kind they were, sort of like the cedar trees at Lebanon, big, tall trees. There wasn't much of a woods, it was maybe an acre, that's all.
Dr: Where was this farm?
Al: Jackson Street.
Dr: Can you tell us some of your other experiences? You worked on a farm?
Al: I used to ride a horse a lot.
Dr: Where did you ride the horse.
Al: On the farm.
Dr: What state was the farm in?
Al: Ohio

NOTE: In Columbus, the author searched state records, found there was indeed a Jackson Street in 1845, but the records did not show who owned the land. It did show a Samuel Carstairs living in Columbus.

Dr: And when you left the farm, where did you go?
Al: Went to school again.
Dr: What did you study this time?
Al: Something about a minister.
Dr: You became a minister?
Al: No. Studied to be one, stopped. Didn't like it.
Dr: And what did you do then?
Al: I was tired of work . . . building houses. This was in Cleveland, Ohio.
Dr: What time was this.
Al: 1858.
Dr: Who was president then?
Al: Lincoln was running for president. Something about Dred Scott.
Dr: And how did you feel about the Dred Scott . . .
Al: I was for Lincoln. I think he's a good man.
Dr: And then what did you do?
Al: I went into the army, against the confederates. I thought that was the thing to do. Down at Bull Run.
Dr: What regiment were you in?

Al: 31st Regiment.
Dr: For what state?
Al: Illinois. I went out to Illinois and I enlisted. The date was March 2, 1860. Decatur, Illinois . . . That's where I went in the front door, and they gave me gray pants, a blue coat, buttons on it, a funny looking hat, street car conductor or something.
Dr: What kind of emblem was on the cap? Examine the cap closely.
Al: It had an arrow pointing downwards through the emblem. "In Union There is Strength," in gold letters, wasn't gold but it looked like gold . . . I went in as a drummer boy, 31st regiment.
Dr: What was your name?
Al: Jack Carstairs. Private Jack Carstairs.
Dr: And you were a drummer?
Al: A drummer boy. I could drum good, too!
Dr: Where did your regiment go from Decatur?
Al: Gettysburg, Pennsylvania. We trained there. Big field. I used to play the drums for marching.
Dr: And where did your regiment go then?
Al: There was a hundred twenty men in my company, B company. We went right into action. Manassas (mumbled) I don't want to think about that. That's awful. Awful lot of people killed. I don't want to . . .
Dr: Would you tell me which battle, of Manassas or Bull Run? There were two battles; which were you in?
Al: Both of them.
Dr: Which one were you wounded in?
Al: Second battle of Bull Run.
Dr: Were you taken to a field hospital there?
Al: Yes.
Dr: What was it like?
Al: It was a tent.
Dr: And how did they treat the wound?
Al: They took alcohol and washed it. It wasn't bad.
Dr: Who was your commanding officer?
Al: Don't remember. Let me see . . .
Dr: Do you remember the names of any of the officers?
Al: Lt. Fred Grant.
Dr: Did they release you out of the army then?
Al: No, I was at Manassas.

Dr: Who was your commander there? Can you recall your officers' names?
Al: Something about a church.
Dr: You see a church? Was this on the battlefield?
Al: No. Big steeple. In Richmond. On Spicer Street. I was in the church.
Dr: Do you recall what time this was?
Al: Three o'clock in the afternoon. It was Sunday.
Dr: And what was the date?
Al: 21st of July, 1864.
Dr: And what happened?
Al: A funeral of some kind.
Dr: Look into the casket and tell us who it was.
Al: My father, Samuel

***

Dr: What was your aspiration?
Al: to commune with God.
Dr: And how did you want to obtain this communion with God?
Al: Study to show thyself approved unto God. A workman is not to be ashamed.
Dr: Tell us about some people that influenced your life during your religious study.
Al: Cardinal something. I can't remember.
Dr: Was he a Catholic?
Al: I wasn't, but he was.
Dr: Where was he located.
Al: Boston.
Dr: Did you correspond with him?
Al: I went to see him.
Dr: Would you describe him to us?
Al: Kind man, loving, peaceful. I wanted to find out what he had to teach me.
Dr: Did you find out?
Al: He made me a Catholic.
Dr: A priest?
Al: No, just a Catholic. I studied and studied but didn't think I could become a priest. I wasn't good enough.
Dr: What did you study? Could you tell us some of the books?

Al: A red book it was. "Walzack". He wasn't Catholic. How did I get hold of that thing? Maybe that's why I stopped being a Catholic.
Dr: Supposing we come to the time ten years before your death. Tell us where you were.
Al: I was 58 (when I died) and that makes me 48. I was in Toronto, Canada. Working in a mill there. Carpenter . . . Lost my arm. Saw cut my arm off.
Dr: Which arm was it?
Al: Right arm. Hurts.
Dr: And you were treated in a hospital or a doctor's house?
Al: Toronto General Hospital.
Dr: Do you remember the doctor?
Al: Dr. Stevens.
Dr: Did the loss of your right arm have a profound effect on you?
Al: I didn't want to work any more.
Dr: What did you do?
Al: I studied.
Dr: What did you study?
Al: Bible.
Dr: Did you believe in Reincarnation?
Al: No.
Dr: You had become a Catholic.
Al: That's right. That's rubbish. I don't believe in that stuff.
Dr: Did the Catholic priest condone your reading the Bible?
Al: I didn't let him know it.
Dr: Were you married at this time?
Al: I was married, yes.
Dr: What was your wife's name?
Al: Sara.
Dr: Where was she living?
Al: In Toronto . . . Belle street, 15.
Dr: When did you marry your wife?
Al: 1860. She was 15 years old.
Dr: Where did she come from?
Al: She came from Philadelphia.
Dr: What were her parents? Dutch?
Al: Chinese.
Dr: Was she accepted in your social group?
Al: No.

Dr: Where did you leave your wife during the Civil War?
Al: In Toronto. I was back and forth to Toronto, Cleveland, Decatur, Illinois—that's where I enlisted.
Dr: Can you tell us more about your wife?
Al: Nobody liked her. She was Chinese.
Dr: But you loved her.
Al: Ming was her name, but I changed it to Sara so people would like her.
Dr: Could you speak Chinese to her?
Al: No. She spoke American.
Dr: Did your wife become a Catholic?
Al: No.
Dr: What was her religion?
Al: She didn't have any. Beautiful little thing. 4'6", brown—black hair.
Dr: Did you have any children?
Al: Yes, two children, Bob and Alice.
Dr: Where was Bob born?
Al: Philadelphia, Pennsylvania
Dr: What was the date?
Al: December first, 1869. Robert Earl Carstairs.
Dr: And where was Alice born?
Al: 1875, in Toronto. She died at birth.
Dr: Did your wife take good care of them?
Al: Yes . . . very, very good. She was sweet.
Dr: Did she sing to them? Did she sing to Bob?
Al: Yes.
Dr: What kind of songs?
Al: Little Chinese lullabies.
Dr: Can you give us the tune of one of those Chinese songs?
Al: (sings "Ling, ling, ling," etc., with a simple, four-note melody.)

***

Dr: Did Bob go to school?
Al: Yeah.
Dr: Where?
Al: In Philadelphia.
Dr: When did he start school?
Al: 1876.

Dr: How long did he go to school?
Al: He went to school five years, and . . .
Dr: Where did he live at the time?
Al: 1212 Spring Garden Street. Then we moved back to Toronto, to Bleeker Street.
Dr: Did you always live in the same house?
Al: No, I moved twice . . .
Dr: Were you ill toward the end of your life?
Al: Never seemed to get sick. Lost my arm, that's all.
Dr: Did you come back into this country after 1890? The U.S., that is.
Al: Lots of times. Buffalo. I used to have a girl there. Shouldn't do that because I was married.
Dr: And what was her name.
Al: Louise. I don't want to talk about that. Shouldn't do that. That's not right.

***

Dr: Tell us where you were living in 1850.
Al: Columbus, Ohio.
Dr: And in 1860.
Al: Two places. I was in Richmond and I was in Toronto.
Dr: And in 1870?
Al: Toronto.
Dr: And in 1880?
Al: Toronto.
Dr: And in 1890?
Al: I was in Boston and I also lived in Toronto.
Dr: And in 1900?
Al: (slurred) I'm on Venus.
Dr: Do you remember where you were in 1895?
Al: Here I passed on.
Dr: Can you recall? If it is unpleasant you don't have to dwell on it.
Al: (heavy breathing) The window. Pneumonia. I'm lying beside the window. My wife is sitting at the bedside. Sara. All of a sudden there is an angel and just—I walked off. That wasn't unpleasant. It was pleasant.
Dr: Can you give us the date when you walked off?

Al: April Second, same date, April Second, 1895. Veasey Street, 4025 Veasey Street, Toronto.
Dr: Where were you buried?
Al: You mean the name of the cemetery?
Dr: Yes.
Al: Gracefield Cemetery.

The questions also elicited information that Jack had lived in New York for a brief period in 1875, at 121 Gramercy Place, on the second floor, while he worked at taking care of horses at Jackson Livery Stable at 5107 Gartner Street. There was also more information on his civil war experiences, including a description of General Sherman: "A tall man, six foot tall, a very stern face, looked like, you say, the wrath of God, like he could slice everybody in two, bushy brows, flashing black eyes, nose that was long, aquiline."

SUMMARY

Jack Carstairs grew up with a stern but loving father, who wept over him when he fell from a tree when he was eight, and who wanted him to follow his business. Jack instead did not continue his education but enlisted in the army at age 15. Later he had an urge to seek union with God, to learn from religious authority. He married a Chinese girl; they had two children, of which one, a girl, was born dead. After a severe accident, he had to stop working. He died ten years later, peacefully, with his wife at his side.

Correspondences with Albert's life include the stern but loving father, who wept over him when Al was struck by a car at age seven; not getting as much education as his family wanted him to; enlisting in the armed forces; marrying; having a daughter dying at birth; desiring religious knowledge and experience; having a severe accident (in the form of a stroke/heart attack) that hospitalized him and made him quit work; the peacefulness of dying with his wife at his side.

PIERRE (about 1710 to 1715)

Late in the first session, Dr. George asked, "Did anyone ever drown where you were?"
Al: I did once, but that was in the previous incarnation.
Dr: Where was that, do you remember?
Al: France.

***

Dr: And what was your name?
Al: March 29, 1710, I was born. Chatil Court. Name was Pierre.
Dr: What was your father's name?
Al: Pierre.
Dr: What was your mother's name?
Al: I can't remember.
Dr: Did you live in the city or the country?
Al: Chatil Court. I can't remember. I can't remember anything!
Dr: And you relax.
Al: Jesus! Jesus! Appeared in a vision.
Dr: He appeared to you in a vision?
Al: I wish, couldn't I repeat that vision? 1715. Five yearsold.
Dr: Can you tell us anything else about your life as Pierre? Remember the country?
Al: Beautiful country. I was killed in an accident. I don't want to remember that. I was five years old. I don't want to remember that! I don't wanna remember that at all!
Dr: Could you say a few words as the people spoke there?
Al: I don't want to remember that! It . . . oh (moans) . . .

SUMMARY
Pierre remembered his father's name, which he bore himself, but not his mother's. He recalled an accident in which he apparently drowned, at the age of five. At that time he saw a beautiful vision of Jesus.

Correspondences with Al's life include being named after his father, and having a terrible accident as a child. (Al nearly died when struck by the car. Pierre did die of drowning.) There was a beautiful vision of Jesus. Al did not report such a vision in his current life, but had many beautiful experiences close to visions.

SON OF JAMES I (about 1585–?)

Dr: Now we would like to have you go back further in your experiences. Would you like to go back to one of your previous ones? When did you live in England? Who was king when you were in England?
Al: James.
Dr: What James?

Al: James First. Wait a minute. 1585. Some relation there . . . James Second. Son of James First. Grew up. 15 years old, I didn't like it. I went over to France.
Dr: What was your name?
Al: James Second. James First was king.
Dr: You were his son?
Al: That's right.
Dr: Who was your mother?
Al: Elizabeth . . .

>NOTE: Elizabeth was the "Queen Mother", without a doubt, as James VI of Scotland carried out his duties until, at her death in 1603, he assumed the English throne as well. The king may indeed have had a son James, but it was his son Charles who ascended the throne as Charles I, and Charles's son, James, who became James II in 1685.

Dr: Who were you with in France?
Al: There was a girl . . . I was 15 years old. It was . . . Mount Carmel in France, just like Mount Carmel in Palestine. It was so beautiful. And she was 15. I'd better not go on.
Dr: Did your father know you were in France?
Al: No, but he found out, and made me come back.
Dr: How did you manage to get away?
Al: We had a son (sigh) . . . and he called me back. On a boat. I was disguised . . . Somebody knew where I was. I went over and hid. I wandered around the countryside. I stayed in Tuilleries for awhile, then went through (something sounded like Saint Sans Froid) and finally to this girl. We had a son.
Dr: What was the son's name?
Al: Alan.
Dr: Did he live?
Al: He lived in France, and "Matron" was my wife's name, although we weren't married . . . And that wasn't right either, and she left the boy with monks and she went into a monastery. I went back to England. I do not feel so good now.
Dr: Did you marry when you were in England?
Al: No.
Dr: Did you have any children?
Al: That child by "Matron". Alan. He was raised by the monks. I could never find him! They took him away. (He sniffed, coughed.)

Dr: Who were the great scholars in England?
Al: Francis Bacon. I knew him, I was only a young kid. Chesterfield. There were a great many . . . but I don't feel good.
Dr: You may relax. We'll pass on to something pleasanter. . . . do you remember working, or having anyone work on the scriptures?
Al: Oh, a lot of people, hundreds . . . That's why I guess I had the experience . . . with Matron, because when I came back I just wanted to improve myself. I knew I had done wrong . . . I had 450 people doing nothing but translation from German to English.

NOTE: In the first part of the 16th century political and ecclesiastical pressures had forced translators such as Tyndale to move to Germany to continue their work. Certainly the King James scholars translated from what was available in Hebrew and Greek records.

Dr: What did you work on?
Al: Translating the Bible, helping helpers. Everybody was working on it.
Dr: Could you read Hebrew?
Al: No. I just got the people to do the work, located the scholars.

SUMMARY

James, son of James I, ran away from family and father's influence at age 15, to France. There he found a sweetheart, had a son—but lost sight of his child and his mate as well. Brought back to England by his father's men he was later involved in religious work in the sense of helping the Bible translators.

Correspondences include: bearing his father's name, feeling he had done something his family disapproved of, leaving home—but at age 16, not age 15—to look for another kind of life as he hitchhiked to California. So far as we know there is no son he lost sight of, but we have no way of knowing whether his misadventures in Haiti included anything of that nature. There was of course considerable Bible study, also working with the Bible and readings, but not translations.

JESUIT PRIEST (about 1450)

Dr: . . . Bring up what you remember.
Al: Fourteen hundred and fifty. As a monk. Italy. Name (whispers) I can't remember.

Dr: What part of Italy were you in?
Al: Naples. But I didn't stay there long.
Dr: Do you remember the order?
Al: I . . . something about columns. Down the mountain.
Dr: Do you remember anything else? Did you wear a black robe, a brown robe or a gray robe?
Al: Black robe, black robe.
Dr: Were you a Jesuit?
Al: (voice of authority) Yes.
Dr: Were there many Jesuit priests at that time?
Al: There were twenty of us in that order. Friar, they called me.
Dr: Who was the Pope at that time?
Al: Leo.

NOTE: Leo X was elected Pope in 1513, when this Friar, if born in 1450, would have been 63 years old.

Dr: Was the church at war with the State?
Al: Church and State were united, all together.
Dr: What else did you do?
Al: I didn't stay with other monks anymore.
Dr: Did you go live by yourself?
Al: Yes, I did, far away from . . .
Dr: Did you know Savonarolla?
Al: I didn't meet him. I knew that name.
Dr: Was Michelangelo there?
Al: Michelangelo, painter. I watched him paint one time.
Dr: Where was he working?
Al: Venice, along the water. Painting, painting a madonna. Brown color—halo, blackish hair. Beautiful painting. Days he spent, weeks.
Dr: Was it in a chapel?
Al: No, he was painting it along the water . . .
Dr: Can you give us some of the ritual you used in your order?
Al: It isn't allowed to give. (For the next three questions, about the head of the order and such, Al did not answer.)
Dr: Did you pray a lot?
Al: All the time.
Dr: Would you repeat some of your prayers for us?
Al: Laude, laude, Patrem . . . I feel like I'm in between somewhere and somewhere else . . .

SUMMARY

The Jesuit Priest gave himself to his work as a priest, but did break away from the regular group to go out on his own later. Religious study is the major correspondence here.

THE HAPPY TRIPOLITAN WACHWA-WACHWA (about 929–956)

Dr: And will you go back further for us? Tell us what you see?
Al: Umm—umm . . . 952. Tripoli. I was colored. Heat, many sands.
Dr: What was your race?
Al: Tripoli, Tripolitan, Black race. Sand all over the place.
Dr: Were you married?
Al: No. no interest. (He began talking with a rhythmic resonance.) Yung bung jong-ing.
Dr: What does that mean?
Al: Lots of people all over, we're all having a time. We don't work, just sing.
Dr: What religion were you?
Al: Don't have any. I'm not interested in any of that . . .
Dr: Are you a slave?
Al: No, I'm not a slave. We just have a good time.
Dr: Were there any musicians?
Al: Oh, yeah . . . With zithers and harps . . .
Dr: Any others?
Al: Oh, a lot of others. We had drum made of camel skin.
Dr: What kind of weapons did you use?
Al: Bow and arrow, but I didn't fight, when we could sing.
Dr: Will you sing a song for us?
Al: It's too hot to sing, we only sing in the cool night time.

The doctor eventually peruaded him to sing a song, which he did with great abandon. In the next session, the doctor leads him back to the Tripolitan life.

Al: Oasis, and you get a drink of water if you want any. There's a whole lot of little huts a long ways away, palm trees growing near, a whole lot of them, must be fifty. We're sitting around all together. It's cool, because the Mediterranean Ocean has breezes from the north. Some fellow has a harp and he's playing . . . Isn't that pretty?
Dr: Beautiful.
Al: I wish I could sing like the other fellows do.

Dr: You sing beautifully.
Al: It's so pretty. The stars, it seems like you could just reach out over the stars, and the boys all singing . . . and we sleep right out in the sand.

Longo, he's the leader of us, he's a big, black man, sort of a gold beads around a . . . funniest looking thing, with his hair knotted up. He's going to start the next Aliman, Aliman, that's the name of it. (Al sings a song, "Nocha, nocha, aliman, nocha, nocha, aliman . . .") Hey, Longo, that's pretty! . . . Aliman means twilight stars. The stars will always gleam in the hearts of men . . . I'm of the tribe, Longo is our leader, the tribe of Nocha.

Dr: Where do your people come from originally?
Al: You mean where was I born?
Dr: And where did your father and your father's father come from?
Al: Egypt, we came from Egypt, long line of descendants. We were slaves. We got away, we got to Tripoli. We don't want to fight, we don't want to be slaves and work, just sing. (Sings "Aliman, Aliman, Nocha, Nocha".) . . . See, we all got out of Egypt when we were young. I remember when a little boy my father getting whipped with red welts on his back, 'cause he wouldn't row some princess down the Nile hard enough and she beat him. I said, 'Oh, boy, I've got to escape!' Then these people adopted me on the desert. I didn't want to have anything to do with any women after that. . . . we don't want any women here in this land. All they want is jewels and persecuting men. We're happy, in Longo tribe. The Creator has given power to this tribe to make men happy. Longo is greatest. He plays the zither and we sing. (On request he sings a similar song, loudly and happily.)
Dr: What do you eat?
Al: The leaves of the trees, mangoes, fish. You just walk in (the Mediterranean) and pick them up. Net them. Plenty to eat. (Later he burst into another song.)
Dr: That was a fine song. What does it mean?
Al: We take of God's will and make it into joy. The joy we have is today, today is ours. That's all. It's in the language of Nubian, that is the name of the language we used.
Dr: Will you tell us how you met your death when you were with Longo?

Al: 27 years old, 956 A.D. Swimming, not too far out, fish, big fish, I guess shark, bit off leg, right below the knee cap.
Dr: You need not dwell on that.

SUMMARY

As a child, Watchwa escaped with others from a woman who beat men too hard. He found physical and spiritual delight on the beach with many friends, under a leader he loved, with music, singing, dancing. The whole group preferred peaceful living to fighting. The philosophy was summed up in that song, "We take of God's will and make it into joy. The joy we have is today. Today is ours." However, he died quickly and violently in the water.

Al, too, found at least spiritual delight at Virginia beach with many friends, people he loved. He helped initiate the Friends' Meeting there; Friends are firm in preferring peace to fighting. The taking of God's will and making it into joy was what he was actively doing, much of the time, at the Beach. His frequent greeting, "Happy Birthday," was based on the belief each day brings a new chance, a new life, very similar to "Today is ours."

PETER/GREGOR IN SIBERIA (about 820)

Al: It's cold, bitter cold. 820 A.D.
Dr: That was your next incarnation?
Al: No, it's the one I'm in now. Siberia. It's 50 below zero.
Dr: How old are you? And your name.
Al: 42. *Peter*. (In earlier session, he gave his name as *Gregor*.)
Dr: What language do you speak?
Al: I have a language you do not know, called the Semin, used by those tribes of eskimoes in northernmost Siberia.
Dr: And what are you doing there?
Al: Freezing. Freezing to death. I can't move.
Dr: Why are you freezing to death there?
Al: I'm lost from my tribe. I fell into a glacia deposit. It's cold, awful cold.
Dr: Can you go back a few years in your life to when you were a young man?
Al: 807 A.D., a town 475 miles north of what is now Vladivostock. We live below ground. Our homes are deep underground. It's the only way we can keep warm.

Dr: What do you wear?
Al: Fur, fur of the Arctic munst. It's a large animal, looks like a leopard. I've got one coat made of rabbits.
Dr: How do these people live, in families, clans?
Al: We live in tribes. There are 120 of us, underground we have each a little room, coming up by stone stairs. . . . What are you doing here, Gregor, somebody asks me. I got to work it out. What? Work out your Karma, Gregor, don't you know that? You've got to go through this life with suffering. Jesus showed us the way, and you've got to do it too. You're going to die, Gregor. It's 50 below zero.
Dr: And do you die at 50 below zero?
Al: Yes, it was good riddance of that body. It was tough.

SUMMARY

The life of Gregor/Peter was one of struggle and suffering, although with the knowledge that Jesus had shown the way. He also knew that the spirit could get rid of a poor body, and seemed glad of the opportunity.

Correspondence with Al's life would include his physical struggling with bodily infirmities, and knowing Jesus had shown the way.

STRONGES, THE ROMAN SOLDIER (about 201–280 A.D.)

Al: The year (of birth) 201 A.D. The name, Stronges. In Rome, Italy. Born a bastard, from the Pope. I'm an illegitimate son of the Pope.
Dr: Who was the Pope, your father?
Al: Clementhow. Short name was Leo first.
 NOTE: There was a Greek Christian theologian, Clement, 150–220 A.D. Pope Leo I, however, lived more than 100 years later, 390–461 A.D.
Dr: Were you a Roman soldier?
Al: Yes . . . We had the Aryans to fight with. The only way to get rid of them was to kill them, and we did it. Later on. . . . We speared them. I was in a battle . . . the battle of the plains, in 256, in the Mesopotamian plain. More than 400,000 people were killed.
Dr: And were the Romans victorious?
Al: Yes. Every man was killed on the field. It was the only way Christianity could win. Kill them all, all non-believers.

Dr: Your general is a Christian?
Al: Yes, he was Christian, he believed in the Holy Trinity. These other people don't, so we kill them all.
Dr: And that was the accepted faith of Rome?
Al: Yes Christianity, I accepted it now.

NOTE: From about 40 A.D., Christians were sometimes accepted, sometimes persecuted in the Roman Empire, depending on the local commander and on the area. Not until Constantine, after crediting the Christian God with giving him victory in battle, made it the "official" religion of Rome, were Christians more likely to take over as the soldier described it. This was somewhere around the year 310, or 54 years after the date mentioned by "Stronges."

Dr: Do you as a Roman soldier believe in the resurrection?
Al: Resurrection of what?
Dr: Of the Christ?
Al: I don't understand it. There is only the doctrine of Father, Son and Holy Ghost. Amen.
Dr: Tell us about the coins which you used as a Roman soldier?
Al: There's somebody.
Dr: Tell us who you see.
Al: Blue eyes, the year 232, the place, Venice. Someone is there, so beautiful. It is she whom you know as Gladys Davis, in 1952. The year 232 her name is Brunhilde. She is Viking, blond hair.
Dr: And what was her religion?
Al: She was a Christian.
Dr: Did she try to convert you?
Al: Wasn't interested . . . but she did.
Dr: Did you have children by her?
Al: One child, male.
Dr: Does that personality carry over? Have you known him in any other incarnation?
Al: Knew him in Egypt as Ra Ta, 20,950 B.C.
Dr: And what was his name?
Al: We had a son, his name was Paul.
Dr: Was he named after the apostle?
Al: Yes, he was. I named him.
Dr: Did he become a soldier?
Al: No, he was a builder. He taught people how to build. He was a follower of Socrates. He taught people, he had hundreds of people come to (hear him) speak. I did not see much of him.

Dr: And when and where did you die?
Al: 280 A.D., in Sicily.

SUMMARY

Stronges led a military life, casual about religion—He was brought to Christianity by the Viking, Brunhilde. He had a son, Paul, a fine speaker whom he did not see much of.

Correspondences include fondness and admiration for a Paul, whom he did not see enough of and a love for a beautiful woman, Gladys, who exemplified Christ-qualities for Al.

ACHMESH

Dr: All right. You can go back, you're going back. Now tell us what you see.
Al: There is a storm coming up.
Dr: What kind of storm?
Al: Awful storm. The sky is very black. I am watching.
Dr: Where are you watching from?
Al: You can see it as easy as I can. An awful storm. Earthquakes.
Dr: Does the ground shake?
Al: Shaking all over. It's just awful, awful.
Dr: Where are you?
Al: Place called Golgotha, and the sky is awful!
Dr: What are you doing at Golgotha?
Al: Standing watching. There's a whole lot of people. All dressed in funny kinds of robes. Dirty, filthy people. Dust and . . . they got all kinds of . . . Oh, it's awful. One fellow has a red . . . around his shoulders. They're running, running, running. I don't know what it's all about. Storm, thunder and lightning. Everybody's scared.
Dr: But there have been thunderstorms at Golgotha before. Why should they be afraid of this storm?
Al: Something has happened. Something about a man. Everybody is rushing by. Filthy dirty, ooh! (He makes spitting sounds, as if spitting out dirt.) What dirty people!
Dr: Are they clean-shaven?
Al: No, they've got beards, filthy, dirty. Running, afraid of the storm. So much noise. You can see them.
Dr: Tell us what has happened.

Al: Awful noise, I'm scared too. I don't know why—I stand there watching these people, filthy . . .

Dr: Is it a high hill, Golgotha?

Al: Yes, it's about 150 feet. There's something on top. Three crosses there. All the people are away from it. What are they afraid of? Some woman kneeling at the foot of a cross. Middle, the cross is in the middle. He said, "Father, forgive them, they know not what they do." And there isn't anything else there, just a man bleeding. The side of his face is cut. Nails. Look of compassion. Quite a distance, but it seems like I'm right up. I don't see the people anymore. It's so beautiful. Can't you see it? It's right over there. People are all gone.

Dr: What is your name?

Al: Achmesh.

Dr: What is your tribe?

Al: Israel. Tribe of . . . Don't take me away from that. Storm seems all gone. Seems like he's dead, but he isn't dead. He's not dead. Just smiling. Compassion. A man's coming. Where did all those people go? Where did they go?

NOTE: The above was in the first session. In succeeding sessions Dr. George brought him back to the life of the Hebrew at different times.

Dr: Now will you go back further and tell us about your occupation when you were a Jew?

Al: I used to give water to people who came to the well. It was near Jericho.

Dr: And what tribe were you a member of?

Al: Benjamin.

Dr: And who was king of Israel?

Al: Tribal king? Pontius Pilate was the Roman governor. Every time one of those Romans came, we had to hide. They had spears. They wouldn't hesitate to put them . . . I seen many innocent . . . with spears stuck in them just for sport. We were looking for a king, to deliver us from the Romans. But I just used to haul a bucket up to give people water when they came by.

Dr: Tell us what you remember about Pontius Pilate?

Al: Bald headed. He didn't know anything. Just some . . . monkey that the Emperor sent down.

***

Dr: Can you tell us more about your life?

Al: I was born in two B.C. in a time of travail. Everybody was scared. Everybody was hiding. They were afraid of Herod. He was a monster. He collected everything you had in taxes and left you nothing. . . . My Father's name was Elijah.

Dr: Did you have happy boyhood memories?

Al: Mother's name was Bath. Bath—Naomah.

Dr: Brothers? (he appeared to misunderstand the word 'mother's'. Al did not answer.) Did you have any sisters?

Al: Yeah, one sister. Her name . . . Nacnacima.

Dr: Was she older or younger?

Al: She was five years older than I. She was born seven B.C. When she was twenty, I was fifteen. She was . . . She used to go to the well to get water and take it into Jerusalem. I'm awfully tired.

Dr: You rest, enjoy your memories.

Al: That's who she was, the woman at the well.

Dr: Tell us again?

Al: Oh, you know. My sister was at the well. This man came along and told her she had five husbands. I didn't know that, and she was my sister! And she ran down to Jerusalem. She said, 'The man told me all that I ever knew, at the well!' And I met him at that time but I didn't know who he was. That was the man on the cross that was crucified.

Dr: And what did you do after the crucifixion?

Al: Couldn't move.

Dr: Did you become a follower of this man?

Al: I didn't know what all this was about. I was afraid of all the soldiers.

Dr: How did you support yourself?

Al: Carpenter.

Dr: Would you describe the tools you used?

Al: Hammer of stone. Saw, and we used sand to put rocks together mixed with water . . . hammer, stone chisel and stone saw.

Dr: You worked mostly on stone rather than on wood?

Al: On stone.

NOTE: On July 1, 1952, Dr. George arranged for a man who was familiar with ancient Hebrew, a Mr. Heber Nelson, to help in the session when Al was again regressed to the life as Achmesh.

Dr: What is the date?
Al: 5 A.D. The street is Untwine, Nazareth. I'm seven years old. It's hot. Sand. The street is sand. I'm going in the synagogue. Oh, there's a lot of noise. Doves flying around. People shouting. I don't like this place.
Dr: Will you describe it for me?
Al: It is marble, made of marble comes from Lebanon, and marble steps, and there are people jostling each other. There is a man with a beard, six inches long. It's light and dark brown, light around his chin and then dark brown. His name is David. David Xerthes. He wants to talk to me.
Dr: You speak to him.
Al: He says, (apparently talks in Hebrew) and I say that I don't like the place. I'm going out of it. It makes me sick to see all these people jostling each other. I walked down the steps and go back to my mother. Shalom, Mama.
Nelson: Shalom.
Al: Is that you, Mama?
N: It is a friend. (He speaks in Hebrew.)
Al: Where are you, Mama? I don't know who that is!
Dr: It is a friend, and you will speak with him. You will hear his greeting, and you will speak.
N: (Hebrew greeting.)
Al: (Also in Hebrew.)
[They continue talking in Hebrew for a few minutes.]
Dr: And tell us about your mother. What is her name?
Al: Her name is Naomi. I want to see my Mama now in the tent and she isn't there. I think she went to wash clothes at the water. Oh, there she is!
Dr: You greet your mother.
Al: Mama!
Dr: And how does your mother greet you?
Al: Sunset. Fifteen years old. I'm in the town of Judasat. It was here Solomon came to arrange with many carpenters.
Dr: What are you doing there?
Al: Trying to read the Aramaic inscription on the front of the synagogue. It says [apparently reads inscription in Hebrew]. Oh, look! Rabbi—oh, isn't he beautiful.
Dr: Describe him to us.

Al: Thin, beard, red hair. Goodness, he's got a halo around him. I can see it. And his hair is like fire!
Dr: What is his name?
Al: It's Rabbi Tine (spells C I N E).
Dr: Will you greet him?
Al: Shalom. Master. I don't want to get away from him. He's dressed in black but he seems so ethereal, beautiful. [Al speaks in Hebrew] He's speaking to me. I kneel at his feet. [More Hebrew.] The words over his head stand out. JHVH. I kneel in humbleness, speechless. Sand, and there's the sun coming up. Oh! Oh! Ah! [panting]
Dr: What is happening?
Al: [mumbles]
Dr: You can tell us.
Al: Somebody is there. A whole lot of people following him.
Dr: Following who?
Al: Some man. Red hair. Funny, I can see him right next to me almost and yet he's way, way off and all these people are following him. Can't seem to catch up. Too many people. Let me run awhile. I'm getting closer. Shadow of a cross on the hill, large shadow. Must be a thousand people, and on the other side is the sea of Galilee. [speaks Hebrew.] Thousands of them, all over. I don't know what it's all about.
N: [Hebrew]
Al: [Hebrew] He's left. He got in a boat. Look at all those people. Some are on crutches then jumping up and down, and some fellow is pulling up corn and throwing it all over, he's so happy.
N: What year are you in now?
Al: 32 A.D. By the Julian calendar XIV, July 14. Something happened here today. It's still happening. Maybe I can catch a boat. Oh, there's another one gone. No more boats. I can swim. Yeah, yea, water's cold. It's not far. . . . Oh, it feels good to lie down on the sand. Rabbi, Rabbi. Somebody's calling. They call him Jesus and (panting) oh, I can't stand it to be near him. It's ecstasy! It's too much! Frightening. He's gonna talk. All those people come over in a boat, they're sitting down. Maybe I can hear him. I can get up closer. "Ye have heard that it hath been said by them of olden time, thou shalt not kill or thou shalt be in danger of the judgment, but I say unto you every man who

is angry with his brother shall be in danger of the judgment . . . Whosoever shall say to his brother, thou fool [speaks in Aramaic] . . . Ye are hungry. Give me of that which you have and I will feed you. Peter, how much bread have we? Fifteen loaves. Give it to all the people and they shall eat. Give me the one fish and I will break bread with you and ye shall drink of my blood that ye too may be one even as I am one with the Father . . . It is twilight. Ye have eaten, now eat ye of the spiritual bread that our Father giveth. I and my Father are one . . . I am the life, the light, the bread, the world life, come only unto the Father through me. It is said by them of olden times the Ten Commandments must be kept, but I give unto you a new commandment: Love one another. As twilight deepens, read, rest in the arms of your heavenly Father."

NOTE: Al also describes an earlier period when Jesus was being taught the mysteries by a lovely young woman, Ruth, at Mt. Carmel. Ruth, he said, was at present living in Virginia Beach, Judy Chandler. His Hebrew sister, Nacnacima, today was his friend Wilmer Alice Adams. He described a scene at Jesus's trial before Pontious Pilate, then a scene after his birth when the wise men, Zoroastrians, approached. Then he described the birth, then appeared to be extremely tired: "There are so many things, you've lost me!"

He described other parts of Jesus's teaching in another session.

Al: He said that only through free will may man lose what he has, and not just what he has but his life—he can never find it unless he loses it.
Dr: But you did not believe this?
Al: It is too much for me. I don't understand it.
Dr: Later did you accept this?
Al: Later I still did not understand it. But I saw and felt . . . Here is how I felt: That once I was on a road and it was dusty. There are a lot of people, maybe fifteen, and they are stoning a man.
Dr: Who are they stoning?
Al: Stephen.
Dr: You see this now?
Al: Yes. It is awful.
Dr: Did you rise to Stephen's defense?
Al: Too late. I got there too late. I knew Stephen. He was great. He said, "Achmesh, carry this message: Christ is king. Become

Dr: that which he was and will be. Christ is king. Achmesh, you will get exactly what I get." All the people left him smashed and stoned . . . As Stephen died I held him in my arms, and then I saw Jesus again but it wasn't the same. He was actually there but he wasn't there, and this was ten years after he was crucified. I had to do that then, to carry on Stephen's message. I had to find the man who stoned him.
Dr: And what was your fate:
Al: Glory, glory. They crucified me too.
Dr: Where?
Al: In Judea. 61 A.D.

> *NOTE*: He gave a further description of his feelings at his crucifixion in another session, quoted in the chapter "Many Lifetimes."

Dr: Will there be any records of Achmesh?
Al: The records were placed in the tomb of Jesus, of Achmesh and Stephen.
Dr: Now, you will rest.
Al: The light, the light in the tomb of Jesus . . .
Dr: Have they found this tomb?
Al: No, it is not to be given. The light . . . it's all light, it always will be. I'm tired, I'm tired.

> *NOTE*: In other sessions he gave further descriptions of the stoning of Stephen, of other incidents in the life of Achmesh, of the appearance of Saul, who, despite his open cruelty to Christians, was "thirsting and crying out" in his soul.

SUMMARY

Achmesh, born in 2 B.C., grew up as a simple Hebrew lad, not educated but wanting to be. His sister had a great experience with "a Man" at the well. He saw Jesus, was fascinated by what he saw and heard. He stood far off to watch the crucifixion, apparently unaware of who and what it was but very aware of the dust and dirt in the air and the terror of the storm. He was persuaded to take the message of Jesus around by Stephen, whose death he witnessed. He reached such spiritual euphoria that when he, himself, was crucified he felt only ecstasy.

The correspondence here seems to be in the feelings of awe, the association of light and holiness, the experience of heavenly ecstasy.

ONON or *ON*
This life turned up when Al, speaking as Achmesh, the Hebrew, recalled that he had helped Solomon put in trees from Lebanon on Mt. Carmel.

Dr: You knew Solomon?
Al: Yes, I knew Solomon.
Dr: Will you go back to the time of Solomon.
Al: Ships we took then on, of Tyre, we had 42 ships. In them we took a thousand trees. Just to put on Mr. Carmel. Solomon told me in that period, I was On, that there was a man, going to be born, who would save the world. He would become the Christ. I told Solomon he didn't know what he was saying. I seemed to be a doubter . . . Solomon said he's built the temple, and one day he says, On, there will be a man who will come in this temple and his feats (the typist spelled 'feets') will be preserved for all time . . . and he will be the Christ.
Dr: What was your name when you were with Solomon?
Al: On . . . Onon.
Dr: Were you a worker in the temple?
Al: No, Viceroy . . . What you call vice-consul.
Dr: But you saw Solomon and you saw him work.
Al: I saw Solomon, and I spent a great deal of time with him. He's quite a man but he had too much knowledge and it went to his head.
Dr: Now tell me, with what did Solomon pay his laborers?
Al: Rolio . . . A rolio equals five shekels. They got one rolio a week.
Dr: What was the symbol, what was on the face of the Rolio?
Al: I see Solomon. On his drawing was a beard, a long beard.
Dr: And on the face of a shekel?
Al: You can find a lot of these in the inner temple, when the temple is opened, August 2, 1958. And Solomon's beard was two feet long, and when this carving was made, and on the other side was the sun, and around the edge of this circular coin are three circles. Inside the circle on the reverse is a dot, representing the sun, coming forth are rays, and the word NUN JOSHU EGEL (something which appears to be) PHROSHNOT.
Dr: What does that mean, PHROSHNOT?
Al: A Galilean word, in Aramaic Watchla . . . means King, Egel

means world, sun, creation, the universe, a . . . lot of things.

NOTE: The words "Watchla" "Walzack" and "Watchwa" seem to have special good meaning for Al in different lifetimes. "Watchwa" was his name during the life in which he experienced so much happiness with song and dancing, in Tripoli; "Walzack" was the name of the religious book which deeply influenced Jack Carstairs. And here, he describes "Watchla" as meaning 'King'.

Al: . . . Solomon's . . . shaved his beard. There are a lot of funny things. I remember one trip to Lebanon. The smell of those cedar trees was sweet. We were lost in the Mediterranean Sea, went up to Cyprus, and a storm—I don't want to talk about that.

SUMMARY

On or Onon gave few details of his growing up. He was a viceroy, or type of counsel to Solomon, handling commercial and trading details. He heard of the coming of a future king but tossed the idea aside. He apparently perished in a Mediterranean storm.

The correspondences here would seem to be in his work, handling commercial and trading details.

Overall, each of the lifetimes to which Al was hypnotically regressed found some resonance in his twentieth-century life. Each was part of the total sum. Each contributed to his journey towards the Light.